THE EXECUTION REVOLUTION

WHY MOST STRATEGIES FAIL AND THE CURE FOR SLOW EXECUTION

JOHAN GRÖNSTEDT

T0243944

Published by
LID Publishing
An imprint of LID Business Media Ltd.
LABS House, 15-19 Bloomsbury Way,
London, WC1A 2TH, UK

info@lidpublishing.com
www.lidpublishing.com

A member of:

businesspublishersroundtable.com

Printed and bound in Great Britain by Halstan Ltd
ISBN: 978-1-915951-45-8
ISBN: 978-1-915951-46-5 (ebook)

THE EXECUTION REVOLUTION

WHY MOST STRATEGIES FAIL AND THE CURE FOR SLOW EXECUTION

JOHAN GRÖNSTEDT

MADRID | MEXICO CITY | LONDON
BUENOS AIRES | BOGOTA | SHANGHAI

CONTENTS

PART II: EXECUTION
74

BAREFOOT IN
THE BOARDROOM

Imagine standing at the starting line of a marathon, surrounded by a sea of determined faces. The air is charged with excitement, each breath you take infused with the collective energy of thousands. The starting line stretches out before you, a thin strip of anticipation that separates the now from the not yet. Each participant poised on the edge of a journey that will test their strength, determination and grit.

But as you glance down, a cold realization dawns on you. You're standing there in socks – just socks, no shoes. Glaringly underprepared compared to the cushioned shoes of your fellow runners. The prospect of running the marathon this way is daunting, filled with the pain of slow, agonizing progress and the inevitability of injuries.

Your competitors, with their high-tech footwear, are not just prepared for the race, but for any terrain it might present. In our rapidly evolving business landscape, clinging to outdated practices is like attempting a marathon in socks. Despite our best intentions, and even when giving it our all, our traditional methods for affecting change are fundamentally flawed, outdated by the relentless pace of today's world. Slow, methodical strategy deployments are relics of the past. If you're clinging to that old playbook, you're on a sinking ship.

I believe that we stand at a pivotal moment. We can either accept the status quo, accepting our staggering rates of failure to reach what is most important in our lives and where we work.

Or we can do something about it. I invite you to the Execution Revolution.

Imagine the potential currently lying dormant within organizations and society – breakthroughs in sustainability, healthcare and technology, all hindered by ineffective execution. It's about ensuring that the next great idea doesn't wither in a drawer but flourishes in the real world, transforming real lives and real communities.

This book serves as a manifesto for this Execution Revolution. It's a toolkit for leaders who are tasked with steering their organizations through uncertain waters. It offers well researched, tried and tested methods for thriving in a world where change is the only constant.

For the leaders of today and tomorrow, this book aims to be what a pair of good running shoes is to a marathon runner: an essential, well-crafted tool that transforms challenges into opportunities for success. For some readers, it will be a wake-up call, a challenge to shift from obsolete methods to modern, effective practices. Because the only managers who will leave a mark in the future are those who can navigate this tumultuous journey. With the help of this book, you will be on track to truly make a difference.

I'm Johan, and I've dedicated my life to the pursuit of excellence within the field of strategy execution.

With more hours invested than I'd care to admit, I've spent my career as a Management Consultant and Chief Strategy Officer. I've carved out a unique path, blending deep theoretical work with rich practical experience. Unlike many in this field who are either academic or practice oriented, I've had the privilege of conducting and refining my research in real-world settings within major organizations. This experience has enabled me to identify what truly impacts strategic success, and what doesn't.

I have consulted with hundreds of senior leadership teams, steering them through pivotal strategic decisions. I've observed these strategies as they unfold across entire organizations, witnessing firsthand their practical application and effects. Rest assured, the methods proposed in this book combine the pinnacle of knowledge in this field with a healthy dose of pragmatic simplification, essential for thriving in the real world.

Through articles, keynote speeches, and now this book, my aim is to inspire and equip a new generation of leaders. This book isn't just a collection of insights; it represents the essence of my lifelong experience, shared with the intention of enhancing our collective ability to achieve our most important goals and aspirations.

Observing the real-world application of strategies has led to an eye-opening realization: our collective approach to strategy execution is deeply flawed. We fail at a staggering rate – nine out of ten strategic initiatives fail to deliver intended value on time,[1] culminating in a projected global loss of $1 million every 20 seconds.[2] It highlights the inadequacies not only of traditional consultancy models but also of in-house 'do our best' efforts.

Both approaches, despite their best intentions, often fall short in driving effective, scalable change across organizations. This challenge points to the need for a more scalable solution, which is where the concept of digital acceleration becomes key. But, despite the widespread digitalization in various sectors, strategy execution has lagged, often confined to basic tools and analogue decision-making processes. This is particularly evident among CEOs, who, despite having access to digital technologies, still mostly rely on fancy Power-Points for critical strategic endeavours.

This book aims to shift this paradigm. It's a manifesto for a new era, one that leverages digital enablement with the pinnacle of modern methodologies to bring strategies to life swiftly, efficiently and with compelling engagement.

STEPPING INTO STRATEGIC EXECUTION

"Without a strategy, execution is aimless.
Without execution, strategy is useless."

– MORRIS CHANG

Morris Chang, founder of Taiwan Semiconductor Manufacturing Company, is a seminal figure in the semiconductor industry and a recognized authority on business strategy, known for his impactful insights at MIT and global leadership forums.

This quote perfectly encapsulates the essence of this book and the methodology we are about to explore. It highlights the circular dependency between strategy and execution, two sides of the same coin, each meaningless without the other.

In this book, we will journey through a streamlined and potent methodology that emphasizes focus, adaptability and speed across the organization. This methodology is further enhanced by digital enablement, making it not just robust but also future-proof and scalable. And it consists of just four easy-to-grasp components.

The first two components, MIGs and Strategic Initiatives, form the strategic part of our methodology. They answer the questions of WHAT we aim to achieve and HOW we aim to achieve it.

MIGs is the art of prioritizing. Exceptional execution begins with narrowing the focus – pinpointing what must be achieved above all else. You can't be everywhere at once, and without this focus, other accomplishments lose their significance. This discipline also delves into how to align goals within a hierarchical structure to maintain focus as you move outward.

Strategic Initiatives is about enabling your focused goals with the most efficient and effective tactics. There are countless paths to the same destination, but it's crucial to chart the most direct course. Overloading on initiatives can dilute resources and blur focus. The key is to select a few high-impact initiatives and nurture them with the full force of the organization's resources.

The third and fourth components, Key Activities and Strategy Stand-Ups, form the execution part of our methodology. They answer the questions of what we DO, in order to focus our efforts and how we sustain change and maintain momentum over time.

Key Activities is about identifying your high-impact actions. It's based on the principle that a small number of activities will drive the majority of your results. It's essential to identify these high-leverage activities and focus your efforts there.

Strategy Stand-Ups is about fostering a culture of commitment and propelling real change. It's a team process that brings to light the successes and failures, enabling course correction and continuous improvement. It's about creating a rhythm of accountability and progress, driving the organization toward its Most Important Goals (MIGs).

We prioritize our
Most Important Goals
What we want to achieve

That we enable through our
Strategic Initiatives
How we aim to achieve our goals

Channel effort into
Key Activities
What we do

Drive progress in
Strategy Stand-Ups
Turning plans into results

We will uncover the theoretical bedrock of these powerful practices, tracing their roots and understanding why certain conventional management principles may not always be your best allies. We will shine a light on hidden behaviours that, while seemingly well-intended on the surface, can have profound and detrimental impacts if left unchecked.

Before we move on, let me take a few minutes to speak directly to you. I read tons of management books, and to be honest, I'm not a huge fan of their typical style. Although the content is interesting, the presentation often feels overly polished and disconnected from the real, chaotic world of leadership. The case stories of flawless success and brilliant insights from top-tier leaders don't truly resonate with the gritty reality of running an organization, where things are constantly moving sideways.

So, in this book, I'm shaking things up. I'm ditching the polished case studies in favour of a band of fictional characters who'll be your companions through the raw, unfiltered side of strategy execution. They will bring the authentic, albeit often awkward, conversations, the difficult decisions, and the pivotal struggles. This approach is not your typical management book fare, but I'm confident you'll find it more relatable. It's about delving into the essence of what leadership and decision making really look like, without the sugarcoating.

These characters are an integral part of the book's larger vision. This book serves as a personal invitation to a journey of growth and achievement, aimed at those who believe we can achieve so much more. It offers you the chance to redefine your approach to strategy and execution and to unlock the full potential for growth within your organization. The journey ahead is challenging, yet the rewards are significant.

I am dedicated to pushing the limits of what's possible in strategy execution, continually innovating and striving for unparalleled excellence. By joining the Execution Revolution, you position yourself for success. This movement thrives on the collective ambition of individuals like you – leaders who grasp the profound significance of our shared mission.

Your contribution is crucial. Each decision and action aligned with this new paradigm brings us closer to our collective objectives. It's an opportunity to not only to fulfil our boldest aspirations, but also to lay down a trail for others to follow, crafting a world adept at confronting its gravest challenges. This is a call for you to become a beacon within your community, leading by example and lighting a path for others, thus amplifying our collective potential to shape a more capable, resilient society.

Let's not just be bystanders in this pivotal moment in the field of strategy. Let's instead be the trailblazers, the pioneers who looked at the challenges and dared to think differently, to act boldly. Together, we can redefine the future of strategy, setting a new gold standard for what can be achieved.

Good luck, have fun and prepare to learn a lot!

PART I

STRATEGY

Our reality is spinning faster and faster, with disruption lurking around every corner. The ability to swiftly decide on focused goals and align an entire organization toward them is no longer a luxury, it is the difference between barely surviving and fully thriving.

Navigating the world of strategic execution is like walking a tightrope. On one side, there's the snail's pace of change, where senior managers grapple with the inertia of lower-level managers, who seem unable to prioritize urgent shifts vital for the company's long-term viability. On the other side, there's the overwhelming whirlwind of initiatives. Senior management, in their hesitation or fear, fail to zero in on what truly matters.

The result is an organization swamped with goals and initiatives, leaving teams overburdened and exhausted. Often, there's the hope that if they just keep their heads down and continue with the status quo, this too shall pass. And then there's the void of accountability. The endless cycle of meetings where commitments are made and then forgotten, promises are broken, and the passionate few eventually leave, seeking greener pastures where their drive is matched.

This will be more than just a theoretical exercise. It's about recognizing that the old ways of doing things may no longer serve us in this new era of constant change.

Prepare for a deep dive into the world of 21st-century strategic planning. Let's set the stage for a journey that will transform not just how we set goals, but how we think about our organizations and the future.

CHAPTER 1

MOST IMPORTANT GOALS AND CHOOSING GREAT OVER GOOD

Chasing goals is like planting seeds in a field of possibilities. Each seed represents an idea, a goal, an initiative. You have the potential to plant all of them, but there's a catch. Your resources are limited. If you try to nourish all of them, some might sprout, but they'll never reach their full potential. They'll remain stunted, their growth hindered by the lack of resources.

Many businesses find themselves in this predicament. They have a multitude of ideas, goals and initiatives, but they struggle with the concept of priority. In today's interconnected work life, many teams and individuals are overburdened with too many, often conflicting, priorities, resulting in a cluttered and stressful environment.

Each new task increases complexity and the likelihood of failing at all of them. It's not just exhausting; it's counterproductive. It's a paradoxical situation where the pursuit of too much leads to achieving too little. A Bain & Company study[3] revealed an astonishing 80% of leaders' time is dedicated to priorities that account for less than 20% of the company's value. This misalign-ment not only exhausts but undermines productivity. Focusing on fewer, more impactful goals ensures mean-ingful progress toward significant, sustainable growth.

"The essence of strategy is choosing what not to do."

– MICHAEL PORTER

Michael Porter, celebrated as the founder of the modern strategy field, is the most cited author in business and economics. His prolific contributions, including 19 books and over 130 articles, have significantly shaped contem-porary business practices and strategic understanding.

This quote by Michael Porter resonates with the principles we are discussing. If you aspire to achieve true success in any endeavour, you need to focus on it. Focus on less to achieve more.

For some reason, many companies seem to overlook this. They acknowledge the concept at face value, but their actions tell a different story. They craft a strategic framework, a road map to success, and invite teams to contribute their ideas, goals and initiatives. This process, known as bottom-up planning, is designed to tap into the collective intelligence of the organization, aligning everyone with the company's strategic direction.

But the process, intended to foster engagement and creativity, inadvertently opens the floodgates of ambi-tion. Teams, eager to contribute, fill the road map with a plethora of ideas. The result resembles a crowded bazaar, teeming with goals and initiatives, each vying for attention – the sheer volume of ideas far outstrips the organization's capacity to execute. *Harvard Business Review*[4] highlighted that only 11% of companies' initiatives are adequately resourced for success. Ambition is disconnected from the ability to execute, leading to a hotbed of stress and unreachable scorecards.

This is where the art of prioritization steps into the spotlight. It's the embodiment of the 'less is more' philosophy, enabling its practitioners to carve out a clear path and maintain direction amid the chaos and clutter. It's the secret weapon that has propelled many to success where others have stumbled.

The ability to focus is the single most important difference between high-performing teams and the rest.

As we delve into this concept, I invite you to keep an open mind. Becoming a master of achieving your goals, whatever they may be, is a life-changing skill. But first, let's establish some fundamental understanding to build upon.

THE EVOLUTION OF GOAL SETTING

"Setting goals is the first step in turning the invisible into the visible."

– TONY ROBBINS

Tony Robbins, a transformative life and business strategist, is a #1 *New York Times* international bestselling author. His significant contributions as an author, entrepreneur and philanthropist have influenced personal development and peak performance globally.

Goal setting has always been a fundamental part of achievement since time immemorial, but it wasn't until the mid-20th century that it began to be formalized and studied as a critical component of professional success.

Cecil Alec Mace, a British psychologist, was an early pioneer in this field. In 1935, he conducted the first empirical studies on goal setting. His research revealed that individuals who set specific, challenging goals performed better than those who set general, easy goals. This was a groundbreaking discovery that laid the foundation for the modern understanding of goal setting in the professional space.

As we move toward industrial efficiency, increasing focus was put into processes to optimize productivity, with businesses striving to maximize output and minimize waste. This was the era of Frederick Taylor's 'Scientific Management,' where every aspect of work was measured and optimized.

The Toyota Production System (TPS), developed in the 1940s and 1950s, was a significant milestone in this era. TPS introduced the concept of 'Kaizen' or continuous improvement, where every employee was encouraged to suggest ways to improve processes and reduce waste. This philosophy of involving everyone in goal setting and problem solving was revolutionary and laid the foundation for many modern management practices.

The term 'Management by Objectives' (MBO) was coined by Peter Drucker in 1954. MBO is a process of setting objectives in an organization to give a sense of direction to employees. MBO defines roles and responsibilities for employees and helps them chart their future course of action within the organization. MBO guides employees to deliver their best and achieve the targets within a stipulated timeframe.

"Management is doing things right;
leadership is doing the right things."

– PETER DRUCKER

Peter Drucker, recognized as the 'father of modern management,' was an Austrian-American scholar and consultant whose writings profoundly shaped the management practices of modern corporations. Authoring 39 books, he pioneered concepts like 'management by objectives' and significantly influenced the philosophical and practical aspects of business management.

This quote by Peter Drucker was as impactful in the 1950s as it is today, drawing a fundamental distinction between management and leadership. Management, according to Drucker, is about efficiency – ensuring that tasks are completed correctly, and processes are running smoothly. It's about the 'how' of things. On the other hand, leadership is about effectiveness – setting the right goals and directing resources toward achieving them. It's more about the 'what' and 'why' of things.

In the 1960s, Edwin Locke popularized the work of Cecil Alec Mace by bringing his thinking to the professional space. Research into goal setting and motivation in the workplace began to gain recognition. Locke's evolution of Mace's thinking came by clarifying the key aspect of commitment and teamwork. Employees may be more committed to a goal if they are part of setting the goals and deadlines.

During the 1970s, SMART goals were introduced. SMART is an acronym that stands for Specific, Measurable, Achievable, Relevant and Time-bound. This framework helped businesses create more effective and achievable goals.

The 1980s and 1990s saw the rise of the famous management adage, "What gets measured gets done." This phrase encapsulates the trend of the time, which was a focus on quantifiable metrics and key performance indicators (KPIs). The idea was that by measuring and tracking specific metrics, organizations could improve their performance and achieve their goals. This trend was driven by increasing workplace digitalization, which made it easier to collect and analyse data.

As businesses grew more complex, a more comprehensive approach to goal setting was needed. This led to the development of the Balanced Scorecard, developed in the 1990s by Robert Kaplan and David Norton. The Balanced Scorecard framework proposed that businesses should measure performance from multiple perspectives, not just financial output. It emphasized the importance of setting goals related to customer satisfaction, internal processes, and learning and growth, in addition to financial performance.

This holistic approach to goal setting and measurement marked a significant shift in management philosophy. It recognized that businesses are complex systems and that focusing on a single metric could lead to unintended consequences.

Parallel to these developments, there was a significant shift in management styles. The 'command and control' style of management, characterized by a strict hierarchy and top-down decision making, was gradually replaced by a more collaborative approach. Managers began to see the value in involving employees in goal setting and decision making, recognizing that those closest to the work often have the best insights.

However, this shift toward a more collaborative approach has not been without its challenges. In some cases, the pendulum may have swung too far, leading to a lack of clear direction and accountability. Striking the right balance between collaboration and leadership is a constant challenge for most modern businesses.

In the 21st century, there has been a shift toward a more balanced and holistic approach to goal setting. This approach recognizes that while measurement is important, it's not the be-all and end-all of goal setting. Instead, modern goal setting focuses on setting ambitious but achievable goals, and then developing a clear plan to achieve those goals. It also emphasizes the importance of flexibility and adaptability, recognizing that goals may need to be adjusted as circumstances change.

Today's highly successful companies understand that goal setting is not just about setting targets, but also about creating a vision for the future and inspiring their employees to work toward that vision.

"A great leader doesn't only inspire us to have confidence in what THEY can do. A great leader inspires us to have confidence in what WE can do."

– SIMON SINEK

Simon Sinek, a distinguished motivational speaker and author, is best known for his concept of 'Start with Why,' which revolutionized thinking in leadership and organizational success. He is the author of several influential books, including Start with Why and Leaders Eat Last, both global bestsellers. His insightful TED Talk on the concept of WHY is one of the most-viewed ever.

The rise of AI and big data has reshaped the landscape of goal setting and strategic planning. These technologies have been offering insights and analytics that savvy businesses have leveraged to make informed decisions, prioritize their efforts, and meticulously track their progress toward their goals.

The history of goal setting in the professional space is a story of evolution and adaptation. It's a tale of moving from industrial efficiency to holistic measurement, from command and control to collaborative leadership, and from rigid plans to flexible tactics. As we navigate the complexities of the modern business world, let's strive to not only do things right but to do the right things. Measure what counts and prioritize what matters.

"The greater danger for most of us lies not in setting our aim too high and falling short; but in setting our aim too low and achieving our mark."

– MICHELANGELO

Michelangelo, a Renaissance icon, profoundly influenced Western art and thought with his mastery in sculpture, painting, architecture and poetry. His diverse talents marked him as a quintessential Renaissance man and his legacy continues to inspire culture.

THE ART OF SAYING NO

The boardroom, usually a place of decisive action and clear direction, was a battlefield of indecision and ambiguity. The management team sat around the polished mahogany table, frustrated and resigned. It had been a long day, fuelled by too much coffee, and the arduous task of reconciling conflicting priorities from various departmental agendas into a unified strategy. Business plans and initiatives lay scattered across the table, each potentially holding the future of the company.

Amid the chaos, the CEO sat as an island of calm, his gaze fixed on the cityscape beyond the window. A man usually known for his decisive leadership, he looked out of place in this setting. His eyes weren't just seeing the buildings and the skyline; they were looking at a future only he could envision. A future that hinged on the decisions made in this very room.

He pondered Michael E. Porter's words, that the essence of strategy is choosing what not to do. But he couldn't shake off the feeling that Porter was just a theorist. How could his ideas help him now, in this room, with these people?

But the CEO knew the hard truths of business. Execution can't always keep pace with ambition. There would be tough choices ahead.

"When people evade the work of choosing among different paths into the future—then you get vague mom-and-apple-pie goals that everyone can agree on. Such goals are direct evidence of leadership's insufficient will or political power to make or enforce hard choices."

– RICHARD P. RUMELT

Richard P. Rumelt is widely recognized for his expertise in strategic management. As the author of Good Strategy Bad Strategy, he has made significant contributions to the field of leadership and decision making. His work has earned him acclaim as a thought leader in strategic planning and execution.

Rumelt believed that the key to a successful strategy was not in trying to please everyone, but in making hard choices. And so did the CEO. He knew that whatever decision he made would ripple through the corridors of the company, affecting lives and livelihoods.

And so, as he took a deep breath and prepared to speak, the room held its collective breath, waiting for the words that would set their course into the future. He had made up his mind. He knew what he had to do. He had to say no.

"Enough," he stated firmly. "We can't continue like this. We can't even agree on our priorities in this room. How can we expect our organization to excel if we can't even decide on a direction? One option would be to shirk our responsibility, to simply say 'yes' to all these ideas. But the stark reality is, we can't do everything. It's as simple as that. We can't fund it all, and we certainly can't implement all of this at once. We need focus and direction, not just for us in this room, but for our entire company. And that starts here, today."

The CEO's words hung in the air, a reminder of what lay ahead. But there was a sense of relief. Finally, someone had said it. Someone had made the hard choice.

CHAPTER 1
MOST IMPORTANT GOALS AND CHOOSING GREAT OVER GOOD

BUT WHY IS SAYING NO SO CRUCIAL?

Every yes is a no to something else. Every resource allocated to one project is a resource taken from another. Every minute spent on one task is a minute not spent on something else. Saying no is about making choices about where to focus your time, energy and resources.

It's about recognizing that you can't do everything, and that trying to do so will only lead to mediocrity. It's about choosing to do fewer things but doing them exceptionally well. It's about understanding that the key to achieving your goals is not in trying to do everything, but in doing the right things. And sometimes, the right thing is saying no.

"You have to decide what your highest priorities are and have the courage—pleasantly, smilingly, unapologetically—to say no to other things."

– STEPHEN COVEY

Stephen Covey, a respected author and leadership guru, is best known for his timeless work, The 7 Habits of Highly Effective People. His enduring legacy lies in his teachings, which encourage saying no to distractions, thereby enabling individuals to focus on their most vital priorities.

HOW TO PROPERLY FRAME GOALS

The walls were covered with charts and graphs, the most prominent being a line graph displaying the company's most important KPIs – profit, revenue and shareholder value – over time.

"If we simply do tomorrow what we did yesterday, we'll likely stay on our current trajectory. But I don't think we're here to tread water. I know I'm not," the CEO asserted, drawing nods of agreement from around the room. "We're here to outpace our market, a feat that, as we all know, is achieved by just 8% of companies," he reminded everyone, referencing a McKinsey report[5] they had recently dissected.

He pointed to the graph, "This line represents our realistic trend, assuming all else remains the same. But our strategic budget, our ambitious three-year plan, is significantly higher. The gap between these two lines is our challenge. Our job is to identify the bets we need to make to bridge this gap."

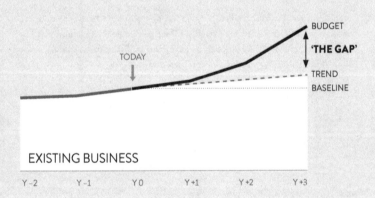

The room was silent, the gravity of the task sinking in. The CEO continued, "If I were to go on vacation for six months, my honest bet is that we would likely continue on trend, our operations largely intact. But without strategic intervention, our chances of outperforming our market are slim."

He paused, letting his words linger before continuing, "Our focus, as the C-suite, should not solely be on managing the current business. We need to create clarity on the difference makers for the future. We need to understand what it will take to move from our current trend to our strategic budget."

The CEO's words resonated with the insights from the McKinsey report, *Strategy to Beat the Odds*, which underscored the significance of making bold strategic moves. The report highlighted that a small, manageable number of strategic levers could account for more than 80% of the variance in corporate performance. It suggested that the key to outperformance was not in making incremental changes, but in identifying and pulling these high-impact levers.

The CEO's message was clear: To bridge the gap between the current trend and the strategic budget, the team needed to identify these high-impact levers within the company and make the bold moves necessary to pull them.

The CEO concluded, "Our task is not easy. It requires us to challenge our assumptions, take calculated risks and make tough decisions. But if we succeed, we will not only meet our strategic budget, but we will also position ourselves to outperform our market. That's our job. That's our challenge."

THE ROLE OF THE C-SUITE

In many organizations, incremental improvements are almost a given. They are the result of competent professionals doing their jobs effectively, guided by established processes and systems. These incremental gains contribute to a company's natural evolution and are often what keeps the organization on its current trend, combined with their underlying market growth.

However, the role of the C-suite is distinctly different and far more strategic. Their primary responsibility is to provide direction that won't materialize organically. It's not merely to oversee incremental improvements, but to identify and act upon leverage points that can significantly shift the company's trajectory.

In essence, the C-suite's role is to ensure that the organization doesn't just evolve but leaps forward. Great senior leaders create unparalleled clarity around these 'difference makers' for the future. While incremental improvements are necessary and happen naturally, significant shifts require strategic intervention. And that intervention is the C-suite's primary responsibility. It's not just about managing what's already working; it's about envisioning what could be and then making it happen.

THE MOST IMPORTANT GOAL

The CEO sat down and leaned back in his chair, his gaze meeting the eyes of each member of his management team. He said, "Last year, we united around six company goals. Six. Now, let's think about what happens when we cascade these goals down through our organization. At each level, we ask teams to align, fill in templates and the like. Each level has to interpret the goals coming from above, and make them their own. But they usually add their own priorities into the mix."

He paused, letting his words sink in. "I've seen teams running balanced scorecards of 17 goals. Do we really believe this team has the right platform to excel? I think we all know the answer. We've seen the struggles in our personal lives from stretching ourselves too thin, but we fail to see the same thing here at the office."

Each of the management team nodded as they absorbed the CEO's words. He continued, "We have goals coming from many directions. Owner demands, compliance demands, the complexity of our matrix organization, and our general inadequacy to prioritize because saying no to things feels uncomfortable. But the reality is, we can't be everything to everyone. We can't chase every opportunity. We need to focus."

> *"There will always be more good ideas*
> *than there is capacity to execute."*
>
> **– CHRIS MCCHESNEY**

Chris McChesney is an authority in strategic execution. He is best known for co-authoring the influential book The 4 Disciplines of Execution, which has provided actionable strategies for organizations to achieve their goals effectively.

And that's where the concept of the MIGs comes in. It's about identifying those two or three goals that, if achieved, will make all the difference. It's about giving ourselves the permission to focus, to say no to distractions, and to channel our resources toward achieving these goals.

He continued, "The more goals we set, the less attention and resources each goal receives. The result? Mediocre performance across the board. But when we focus on two or three MIGs, we can channel all our resources and energy toward achieving them. And that's when we see real, revolutionary change."

It was a simple concept, but one that held profound implications for how his team approached their work. It was a call to focus, to prioritize and to align their efforts. It was a challenge, but also an opportunity – an opportunity to make a real difference, to drive real change and to achieve something truly remarkable.

He leaned forward, his gaze intense. "Priority and direction need to come from the top. It's our responsibility. Nobody else has the mandate to prioritize. Nobody else can see the full picture. And we need to be clear about what our MIGs are."

The CEO brought up the MIT report 'No One Knows Your Strategy – Not Even Your Top Leaders.'[6] He outlined the report's findings, explaining how organizational alignment tends to decrease as one moves down the hierarchy. Even at the top echelons, agreement on priorities hovers around a mere 50%. The situation worsens at the front line, where only about 13% of employees have a clear understanding of the company's most important priorities. Given these statistics, it's not surprising that many companies grapple with executing their strategies effectively.

Percentage of employees that know their company's top three core priorities.

51%
Executive team

22%
Middle management

18%
Team leaders

13%
Employees

MIT – No One Knows Your Strategy – Not Even Your Top Leaders

"We need to rise above these statistics. We need to ensure that our MIGs are not just understood by us, but by every single individual in this organization. And this alignment, this clarity, starts with us," he asserted.

The CEO's words hung in the air, a challenge and a call to action. He had laid out his vision, his strategy for focusing the organization's efforts. Now it was up to them to take up the challenge and make it a reality.

THE IMPORTANCE OF FOCUSED GOALS
AND ALIGNMENT

There are two reasons to focus on just a few MIGs: resource allocation and organizational alignment.

Limited resources mean you can't chase every goal effectively. By narrowing down to two or three MIGs, you allocate resources where they matter the most, increasing the odds of success.

Secondly, alignment is key. The MIT report underscores your baseline, where understanding of a company's strategy decreases down the hierarchy. Fewer, clearer goals make it easier to align everyone in the organization, from top to bottom.

In short, MIGs help you use your resources wisely and ensure everyone is on the same page, increasing the likelihood of achieving your objectives.

A CHALLENGE ACCEPTED

As the CEO's words resonated in the room, a subtle shift at the far end of the table drew everyone's attention. Margaret, the Chief Operations Officer, was not just a force to be reckoned with, but also a warm presence that brought comfort to her team. Margaret had a gift for slicing through the noise and reaching the heart of the matter. Her insights had repeatedly guided the team through labyrinthine challenges. Today, she was ready to lend her voice to the discussion.

She turned to the CEO and said, "I'm with you. We've been stretching ourselves too thin, chasing too many goals at once. We've lost sight of what truly matters."

Margaret had always seen goals as a compass, pointing to the most significant improvements the organization should strive for. Although the organization needed to track a multitude of metrics and KPIs, it had blurred the lines between measuring and goal setting. What needs to be monitored versus what actively needed to be driven forward. Just because they could measure something didn't mean it should be a goal.

"Not everything that can be counted counts."
                                                    – **EINSTEIN**

Albert Einstein, one of history's greatest physicists, left an indelible mark on the world of science. His holistic perspective emphasizes the interconnectedness of knowledge and the significance of qualitative aspects, making his voice a interesting source of inspiration for leadership and decision making beyond the realm of science.

It was up to them to discern the difference as they charted their organization's future course.

"I've been in touch with the team that had 17 goals last year," Margaret continued. "They've been open about their struggles, about the lack of clear direction from us. They've tried to juggle too many balls at once, and have felt the strain. One of them even said that it was like we purposefully set them up to fail. That hit me really hard."

Margaret leaned back in her chair, a sense of relief washing over her. She had been advocating for this change for quite some time. "The concept of the MIGs is potent. It's about prioritizing, about making difficult choices. But it's also about clarity, about providing our people with a clear sense of direction. That's something we've been missing."

Margaret then proposed some ground rules for working with MIGs from a team perspective:

- **Critical Importance:** MIGs are not just any goals; they are the select few that are critical for business improvement. These are the goals that, if achieved, will have the most significant impact on the organization's success.
- **Less is More:** The principle of 'Focus on Less to Achieve More' guides the selection of MIGs. Limiting each team to 2-3 MIGs ensures that resources and attention are not spread too thinly, increasing the likelihood of successful execution.
- **Hierarchical Alignment:** Each team's MIGs should be directly aligned with the goals of the team immediately above them. This ensures a focused and coherent strategy as goals cascade through the organization.
- **Accountability and Influence:** Teams should select goals that fall within their direct sphere of influence. This ensures that team members feel accountable for the outcomes, fostering a sense of ownership.
- **Measurability:** MIGs should be measurable, ideally on a monthly basis, and align with the SMART goals framework (Specific, Measurable, Achievable, Relevant, Time-bound).

Margaret had articulated what many of them had been feeling; the need for clarity and focus. In doing so, she had enhanced the CEO's vision, adding depth to the concept of the MIGs. She had proposed a method to cascade these goals throughout the company in a coherent manner, ensuring that as the goals spread outward, they would not become diluted or descend into micromanagement, but would retain their alignment and focus. This was a crucial step toward ensuring that every individual, regardless of their position, understood and worked toward the same objectives.

As Margaret concluded her thoughts, a noticeable shift occurred in the room. The tension that had earlier been present seemed to dissipate, replaced by a sense of understanding and shared purpose. The management team, initially apprehensive, now appeared more at ease with the proposed ideas.

The CEO observed the change in the room. His message had been received and his vision understood. With Margaret's insightful contributions, the path forward seemed clearer.

FROM VAGUE DIRECTIONS
TO CLEAR PATHWAYS

From a company's perspective, prioritizing goals can pose a significant challenge. Many management teams find themselves anchored to the fundamental metrics of revenue and profit. A handful of executive teams might identify a third, highly specific goal, often driven by an urgent need. This could relate to issues such as regulatory changes, cost-saving measures, mergers or cultural aspects.

The best these teams can usually hope for is to articulate their ambitions in a SMART manner. For instance, they might aim to: *"Increase Revenue from $1,200 million to $2,050 million by December 31, 202X."*

However, one could argue that this approach doesn't truly represent prioritization. Almost every action a company takes on a daily basis could, in some way and if one squints enough, contribute to revenue or profit. Even improving the quality of office coffee could boost morale, thus slightly increasing productivity and, ultimately, raise profit levels. Labelling such broad directions as prioritization seems like false marketing. And if you're thinking along these lines, you're absolutely right. This is where the concept of Strategic Initiatives comes into play.

Strategic Initiatives provide a more focused approach to achieving goals. They represent targeted efforts that directly contribute to the company's MIGs. By identifying and pursuing these initiatives, a company can ensure that its resources and efforts are channelled effectively toward its priorities.

A GUIDE TO ORGANIZATIONAL ALIGNMENT

Before we delve into the intricacies of Strategic Initiatives, let's take a moment to understand the flow of alignment within an organization. The decisions made by the management team about the MIGs and their corresponding Strategic Initiatives must be effectively communicated and implemented throughout the organization. It's crucial to remember that each level of the organization faces the same scarcity of resources, making focus and prioritization equally important at every stage. Here's an optimal process to follow:

1. The management team narrows down their top-level goals, typically ranging from 5-20, to a focused set of 2-3 MIGs.

2. The management team identifies the Strategic Initiatives that will have the greatest impact in achieving these goals, typically reducing a list of 30-60 potential initiatives to a targeted list of 3-6.

3. The management team determines which teams should be involved in each Strategic Initiative.

4. Each member of the management team, typically responsible for their own P&L, then engages their respective teams to determine how they can support the overarching goals. This bottom-up approach fosters ownership and engagement. At this level, the goals are interpreted in a way that reflects the team's unique capabilities and contribution.

5. This MIG breakdown process continues through all levels of the organization. Each manager participates in discussions within their management team and then carries the conversation to their own team, fostering focus and clarity at each level.

6. The implementation of Strategic Initiatives often transcends hierarchical boundaries, as not all teams will contribute to all initiatives. The management team usually has a clear understanding of which teams are essential for each initiative. For those involved, the initiative becomes an integral part of the goal discussion and is often seen as an enabler for the goals identified in the MIG breakdown process.

7. Once the entire company has engaged in this top-down and bottom-up process, the management team can take some time to fine-tune the details. This stage also allows for the identification and resolution of cross-functional dependencies.

In upcoming chapters of this book, I'll share real-world examples from my own experiences and provide a toolbox to facilitate these types of workshops within your team. The aim is to enable you to complete a goal-setting session in no more than two hours.

CHAPTER 2
STRATEGIC INITIATIVES AND THE MAZE OF AMBITION

The CEO leaned back in his chair, his eyes settling on Margaret and the CFO, a man named Richard who was known for his analytical mind and strategic thinking. "We've been discussing our goals, and I think it's time we break them down in a more tangible way," he said.

Richard nodded, pulling up a spreadsheet on his laptop. "Our company's overall revenue ambition is to increase revenue from $1,200 million to $2,050 million by December 31, 202X," he stated, his fingers deftly navigating the numbers. "That's a three-year growth ambition of $650 million. More than 70% growth over three years. It's ambitious, and I'm not sure I believe in the later stages of this budget."

The CEO, ever the realist, interjected with a sense of urgency. "Let's face reality. The board has set this target because they believe it's achievable and only slightly outperforms our market. We're currently growing at 5%, while our market is at 8%. The board is questioning why we're losing market shares. They're convinced that with the right strategic bets, we can reasonably boost our growth to 10% next year. If we maintain our momentum and continue making sound choices, we could see a 20% growth in the second year and, potentially, a 30% growth in the third year. It's a bold target for sure, but it's not beyond our reach."

His tone was firm, the underlying message clear – failure was not an option. The board's expectations were high, and they were looking to the management team to deliver. The CEO's words served as a stark reminder of the gravity of their task and the consequences of falling short.

Richard adjusted his glasses, looking at the numbers again. "If we follow that logic, our revenue would look something like this," he said, pointing to the spreadsheet.

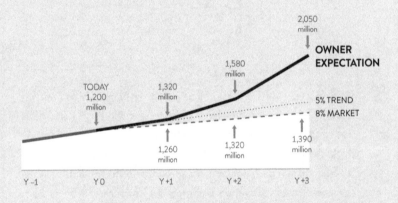

The CEO nodded, taking in the information. "So, there's a significant difference between our trend line and our budget. Our role as a management team is to find the Strategic Initiatives that will enable the extra $660 million that is the difference between our ambition of $2,050 million and our trend of $1,390 million."

Margaret leaned into the conversation. "Well put. Our mission now is to pinpoint the pivotal Strategic Initiatives that will fuel this growth and allocate our resources to them."

The CEO's smile reflected his appreciation for the sharp focus and clarity Margaret brought to the discussion. "Precisely, Margaret. That's our immediate task."

STRATEGIC INITIATIVES

The concept of Strategic Initiatives is not a new one. In fact, it's been around since the days of Management by Objectives (MBO) back in the 1950s. Over the years, it's been known by many names – Must Win Battles, Strategic Pillars, Core Priorities and How-to-Wins. But despite the changing terminology, the essence of the concept remains the same.

At its core, a Strategic Initiative is a tool designed to enable a company to achieve its MIGs. It's telling the company the specific way to achieve the goal, the path to victory. It's the first directional move toward a road map that outlines the steps the company needs to take to reach its destination.

But while the concept of Strategic Initiatives is a universal one, its application can vary widely depending on the specific circumstances of the company. Industry, business logic, market conditions, and a host of other factors can all influence the shape and form of a Strategic Initiative.

Let's explore the more common types of initiatives run by most companies.

NEW VENTURES

When a company embarks on a journey to add something novel to its capabilities, it's venturing into the realm of 'New' initiatives. These initiatives often require substantial investment and a considerable time commitment. However, they can revolutionize the market landscape once they come to fruition. Here are some examples:

1. **Innovation:** The research, development and launch of a groundbreaking product that represents a new generation in its category, promising to redefine customer expectations and set new industry standards.

2. **Expansion:** The strategic expansion into uncharted territories, be it geographical regions or untapped market segments, aiming to capture new customer bases and unlock fresh revenue streams.

3. **Capabilities:** The creation of a new possibility to better serve the market, which could involve the establishment of new business areas or the introduction of innovative service offerings that enhance customer value and competitive advantage.

4. **Mergers and Acquisitions:** This involves strategically acquiring or merging with other companies to expand the company's market presence, diversify its product offerings, or gain access to new technologies and resources. This can be a fast-track to growth, but it requires careful planning and execution to ensure a successful integration and realization of synergies.

LEVERAGE

Within 'Leverage', a company seeks to amplify its competitive edge by capitalizing on its unique advantages in a well-orchestrated manner. These initiatives often represent low-hanging fruit, yet they demand a high degree of synchronization across multiple teams, making them a challenging feat from an execution standpoint. Here are some illustrative examples:

1. **The leverage of size:** This involves harnessing the company's scale to secure a dominant position for larger tenders or to structure deals in ways that competitors cannot match, thereby creating a unique competitive advantage.

2. **The leverage of geography:** This strategy aims to either monopolize specific markets or extract value from a broad ability to deliver services across all markets, thereby winning larger tenders that others can't fulfil.

3. **The leverage of portfolio:** Here, companies adopt a structured growth strategy by maximizing their portfolio footprint among their clients. This ensures efficient cross-selling and optimizes pricing across business areas to combat competition and stimulate growth.

TRANSFORM

In the 'Transformation' category, a company embarks on substantial initiatives to future-proof itself. More often than not, transformation itself isn't the primary value generator. Instead, it serves as a stepping stone, enabling the organization to enhance its competitive edge, foster innovation and stimulate growth in its market, which may currently be hindered by a conventional setup or skillset. Transformation initiatives are typically intricate and demanding, necessitating significant resources and time to execute. However, when implemented effectively, they can yield considerable enhancements in the organization's performance and competitiveness. Here are some representative examples:

1. **Digitalization or Automation:** This involves replacing outdated tools, processes and practices with advanced digital solutions or automated systems, thereby overcoming inefficiencies, and boosting productivity.

2. **Customer Focus or Customer Centricity:** This often entails a cultural shift from an inward-looking focus to an outward one, concentrating all efforts on delivering exceptional customer experiences at every touchpoint. This leads to increased customer satisfaction, loyalty and advocacy, which in turn drive business growth and profitability.

3. **Organizational Redesign:** This encompasses a broad range of hierarchical changes, such as centralizing or decentralizing operations, and introducing or eliminating matrix structures, all based on the market conditions and the need to compete effectively.

4. **One Company:** These transformational initiatives are strategic efforts undertaken by organizations to unify their various departments, teams or subsidiaries under one cohesive identity and operational framework. The goal is to create a more integrated, efficient and collaborative organization that operates as a single entity, rather than a collection of separate units.

SPECIFIC FOCUS

Sometimes, companies find themselves in urgent situations that demand immediate attention and drastic measures. These scenarios often stem from external pressures or strong internal voices, and they rarely arise from a state of harmony. Instead, they are reactive responses to circumstances that cannot continue without significant change. Here are some examples:

1. **Cost-saving Initiatives:** These are strategic efforts to reduce expenses and improve financial efficiency. They may involve streamlining operations, reducing waste

or renegotiating contracts. The goal is to preserve the company's financial health without compromising its ability to deliver value to customers.

2. **Sustainability or Compliance Initiatives:** These initiatives are often driven by new regulations or societal expectations. Companies may need to adjust their practices to meet modern standards or risk penalties, reputational damage or loss of customer trust. These initiatives can involve adopting greener processes, improving data privacy or enhancing corporate governance.

3. **People and Culture Initiatives:** These initiatives focus on the organization's human element. They may involve overhauling leadership capabilities, addressing employee dissatisfaction or tackling issues of safety. These initiatives often correlate strongly with a company's ability to attract and retain top talent. In today's market, a positive and inclusive culture can be a powerful competitive advantage.

4. **Crisis Management Initiatives:** These are reactive measures taken in response to unexpected events that threaten the company's operations or reputation. They require swift action and strong leadership to navigate the company through the crisis and minimize its impact.

Remember, these initiatives are not just about putting out fires. They're about turning challenges into opportunities for growth and improvement, and ensuring the company's resilience in the face of change and uncertainty.

STRIKING THE PERFECT BALANCE: CHOOSING THE RIGHT NUMBER OF INITIATIVES

The principles of prioritization hold true when it comes to selecting the number of initiatives for your company. Remember, initiatives are about channelling resources and directing focus. You can't be everywhere at once, and you can't do everything at the same time. There's a saying that perfectly encapsulates this:

"You can have anything you want,
but you can't have everything you want."

– PETER MCWILLIAMS

Peter McWilliams was an influential figure in the realm of personal development and life strategy. With over 40 books to his name, his work revolved around helping individuals make informed decisions and prioritize their goals effectively.

The number of initiatives you choose ultimately hinges on their financial potential and the ambition of your MIGs. Your task is to identify the levers that will enable you to bridge the gap between your current growth trend and your strategic budget. If you opt for fewer, larger bets, you'll end up with fewer, more focused initiatives. If you choose to pursue incremental improvements, you may need more initiatives. However, managing a larger number of initiatives may be feasible if each one does not require significant change, but keep in mind it often provides less organizational clarity.

Most management teams settle on between 3-6 initiatives for the entire company, although there are valid exceptions. Typically, this translates to 1-3 initiatives targeting revenue, 1-2 addressing profitability, and occasionally 1-2 more that tackle other strategic shifts closely tied to factors influencing company valuation.

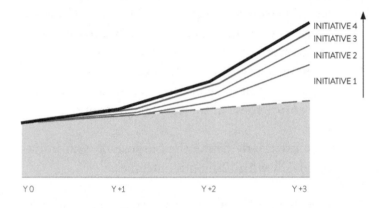

LEADING
WITH PURPOSE

Let's reflect on the crucial role of the C-suite in driving Strategic Initiatives. These initiatives are not just strategic tools; they are the lifeblood of your company's journey toward its MIGs. They are the catalysts that transform your vision into reality.

As leaders, your responsibilities extend beyond merely identifying these initiatives. You are the stewards of your company's future, and it is incumbent upon you to ensure that these initiatives are clearly defined and wholeheartedly embraced by your team.

THE SUCCESS OF THESE INITIATIVES HINGES ON THREE KEY FACTORS:

1. You must identify the Strategic Initiatives that, collectively, enable the achievement of your chosen MIGs, bridging the gap between trend and budget.

2. You must foster a consensus within your management team. Everyone must agree that these are the specific initiatives to focus on, and no alternative initiatives should divert attention from what truly matters.
   - You must prioritize these initiatives above all else. Commit to dedicating your time and effort to ensure these initiatives come to fruition.

3. You must clearly define the purpose of each initiative, ideally with 12-month outcomes.

Without this level of clarity and commitment, your role as leaders is left incomplete. It's not enough to merely set the direction; you must also pave the way and lead your team toward it.

Let this be your call to action. Reflect on these responsibilities. Embrace them. And remember, the journey toward achieving your goals is not a straight line. It's a winding path filled with challenges, opportunities and learning experiences. But with the right initiatives in place and a committed leadership team at the helm, you can navigate this path with confidence and purpose.

In the following chapters, we'll delve deeper into the practical aspects of implementing and managing these initiatives. But for now, let this knowledge simmer. Imagine the possibilities it opens up for your company and your role in shaping them.

*"You cannot hope to build a better world
without improving the individuals.
To that end, each of us must work for
our own improvement."*

– MARIE CURIE

Marie Curie, celebrated for her groundbreaking contributions to science, offers a unique perspective on personal development and growth. While not a traditional voice on strategy or leadership, her worldview resonates deeply with the concept of personal ownership as the driving force behind meaningful change.

THE MANAGEMENT TEAM'S CRUCIAL CHOICES

In the conference room, the management team sat encircled by the remnants of a strategic brainstorming session. The CEO rose, his posture reflecting the day's weight, and scanned the room. His team, with a blend of weariness and resolve, awaited his lead.

He remembered a Peter Drucker quote: "There is nothing so useless as doing efficiently that which should not be done at all," which seemed to capture the essence of their challenge.

He cleared his throat, and said, "We're currently considering over 40 initiatives. This level of diversification is diluting our effectiveness. As we've been discussing, I propose a shift in strategy – focus intensely on two, perhaps three initiatives for each of our MIGs and give them our all."

Richard, the CFO, raised an eyebrow, "I know we've talked about reducing our scope to increase focus, but this is a bloodbath. A lot of effort has already gone into these initiatives."

The CEO acknowledged the challenge, his tone firm yet empathetic. "Our focus should be on making a real impact. We need a revolutionary approach here; what we've been doing in the past is simply not good enough. Spreading ourselves across too many initiatives will reduce our effectiveness. We need to focus on excelling in key areas, rather than having a mediocre spread across too many."

Fiona, the CPO, expressed her concern with a hint of caution, "It's a bold move to narrow our focus. We should prepare for some resistance."

Alex, the CSO, interjected with determination, "Facing pushback is part of the process. What we need are wins!"

The CEO listened intently, acknowledging the concerns. "I understand the efforts put into our current initiatives, but let's reframe our perspective. What if we focus intensely on the initiatives with the highest potential impact? We can quantify their potential with our renewed focus. If we excel in these, we might not need to stretch ourselves thin across multiple fronts."

Richard warmed to the idea, "That approach could maximize our impact and efficiency."

Fiona nodded in agreement, "With the right choices, we might redefine our trajectory."

The CEO summed up, "Let's begin our discussion around our most promising profit initiatives first."

PROFIT INITIATIVES

As the team surveyed the map of 15 profit-enhancing initiatives, Margaret made an astute observation. "Clearly, some of these carry more weight than others. We should focus on big, organization-wide bets that have the potential to impact everyone."

Richard said, "The emphasis on cost savings is crucial. It's not just about spending less; it's about enabling our investment in what truly matters."

The CEO turned to Fiona. "Our Automation initiative is our best bet," she began, "It's more than an efficiency play. It's a much-needed strategic leap that will reposition us for the future."

Margaret added her support, "Automation isn't just cost saving. It's about enabling growth and enhancing our capabilities. Without it, in five years, we'll be irrelevant."

"The investment is substantial, but if managed correctly, it's a step toward a more resilient, future-proofed organization," Richard replied.

The CEO nodded, "This focus aligns with our goal for impactful, targeted initiatives. Everything else must be treated as distractions. Less is more. Are we all in agreement?"

As the discussion drew to a close, the management team felt a sense of unity and clarity. They appreciated the CEO's leadership style, which fostered open dialogue but, ultimately, culminated in clear decisions – they trusted him to make the tough decisions when it mattered the most. The CEO, with his succinct summary of the financial potential of their chosen initiatives, sought one final affirmation from the CFO. Could these two initiatives, combined, meet their ambitious budget expectations? The CFO gave a nod of approval. The decision was made.

REVENUE INITIATIVES

The conversation then shifted toward initiatives that would fuel their growth, and they reached a consensus on the following:

The CEO suggested proceeding with the long-discussed strategic merger. Everyone was convinced that this merger would not only expand their market presence but also introduce advanced technology into their operations, thereby enhancing their ability to provide a top-notch service to their clients. Alex, in particular, was thrilled at the prospect of engaging with a whole new pool of clients.

He put forth the idea of expanding their operations into the UK market, a proposal seconded by the CEO. They viewed this as a crucial move in their quest to become a global powerhouse within their industry, particularly considering the absence of direct UK competitors. Margaret expressed some reservations due to potential operational challenges, but the potential rewards were too significant to ignore. They agreed to tackle any arising issues head-on, as and when they surfaced.

Alex was riding a wave of confidence as the conversation shifted toward revenue generation. He passionately proposed expanding their services within their existing client base, emphasizing the untapped potential of cross-selling and upselling. He knew he needed Margaret on board to provide the necessary structure. Margaret was initially hesitant, but Alex won her over. Fiona and the CEO also endorsed the idea, recognizing the potential it held if executed correctly.

MOST IMPORTANT GOALS	**Increase Revenue**	**Increase Profit**
	from 1,200 million to 2,050 million	from 40 million (3.3%) to 160 million (7.8%)
	Due in 36 months	*Due in 36 months*

STRATEGIC INITIATIVES	**Expansion**	**Automation**
	Financial potential: 575 million	Financial potential: 80 million
	Due in 36 months	*Due in 36 months*
	Merger	**Cost-saving Initiative**
	Financial potential: 220 million	Financial potential: 36 million
	Due in 12 months	*Due in 18 months*
	UK Launch	
	Financial potential: 55 million	
	Due in 24 months	

PURPOSE AND OBJECTIVES

Once you have prioritized your Strategic Initiatives, the next step is to successfully anchor them within the organization and build engagement around the tactics that will help you achieve your MIGs. This is where Purpose and Objectives come into play, serving as the linchpins for strategic alignment and focused action.

Purpose is fundamentally about the 'why.' It serves as a continual reminder of why an initiative was chosen from various strategic bets. This is essential for maintaining alignment and focus, not just at the C-suite level but across the entire organization. As time passes, it's easy for the original rationale behind an initiative to become diluted or forgotten. A well-defined purpose helps to anchor the initiative, providing lower-level managers with a solid foundation upon which to align their teams.

Objectives, in contrast, clarify the 'what.' They set the ambition level for the initiative, outlining what is They set the ambition level for the initiative, outlining what is expected to be achieved and by when. This clarity is crucial for operational alignment, as it helps teams understand the pace and scale at which they need to work. Objectives are the yardstick for measuring progress, offering a benchmark against which the initiative's success can be evaluated.

Together, Purpose and Objectives create a comprehensive road map for each initiative, bridging the gap between strategic intent and tactical execution. They move the conversation beyond buzzwords and generalities, providing a nuanced, actionable picture of what the initiative aims to achieve and why it is vital to the organization's success.

THE FINALIZATION OF
THE STRATEGIC INITIATIVES

"We've laid out our Strategic Initiatives," the CEO began, "now, it's time to give them purpose and structure. Let's begin with our Automation initiative. We need to make sure it doesn't become just another corporate buzzword."

Richard leaned forward. "Exactly. If we don't articulate this clearly, it'll be met with eyerolls across the organization. Automation is so often nothing more than jargon."

Fiona, who had initially proposed the initiative, took the lead. "The purpose of our Automation initiative is to automate routine tasks across all departments to increase our margins."

Margaret considered the implications of Fiona's words and said, "While that speaks to the company's bottom line, it doesn't address the concerns of our employees. We need a purpose that not only clarifies the company's 'why' but also resonates with the people who make this company what it is."

She continued, "Profit margins aren't just about numbers on a balance sheet. It's about ensuring our company's longevity and continuing to invest in our people, our products and our shared success.

"To achieve this, we're making a strategic bet on automation. We believe that by automating routine tasks, we can free ourselves to focus on what we do best and what truly matters. But this move toward automation isn't just about technology; it's about upskilling. It means significant investment in both technology and comprehensive training tailored to each employee's development."

The room felt a subtle shift. Margaret's suggestion felt authentic, and when combined with the clarity of the initiative's objectives, this would serve them well as a platform for communication. The team nodded in agreement; this was a purpose that could inspire action and commitment.

The conversation flowed as they moved on to the other initiatives, each member contributing their insights. The management team understood the importance of investing time and effort into this process. They knew that the payoff would be a set of initiatives that not only aligned with the company's strategic direction but also resonated with the teams and inspired them to action.

As the long day ended, they looked at their work. They had defined Purposes and Objectives across the board. They had distilled their focus down to two MIGs and five Strategic Initiatives, a significant reduction from the previous year's six goals and over 40 initiatives.

The CEO glanced at the clock. The team planned to reconvene for a relaxed dinner in 45 minutes – a brief respite before returning the next day to tackle the next steps. Their work was far from done, but they had made significant strides toward their goals.

*"Progress is impossible without change,
and those who cannot change their minds
cannot change anything."*
– GEORGE BERNARD SHAW

George Bernard Shaw, renowned for his transformative impact on Western theatre, offers unconventional yet thought-provoking insights. Shaw's enduring legacy as an influential playwright and provocative thinker underscores the connection between art and societal change, making his voice a unique source of inspiration for those seeking innovative perspectives beyond traditional leadership and strategy.

CHAPTER 3

SUB-INITIATIVES AND THE PITFALLS OF PREMATURE STRATEGIC HANDOVER

Picture yourself tucked up in a warm hut, sheltered from the biting wind that howls outside. Flickering flames from the fireplace cast dancing shadows in the room. Spread out in front of you is a map of the Arctic, its vast white expanse untouched and unknown. The North Pole, a blank spot on the paper, beckons you with its icy allure. It's a place of mystery and prestige, a beacon that has captivated your dreams and now consumes your waking hours. Your heart pounds a steady rhythm of anticipation and fear. A chill runs down your spine as you trace potential routes with your finger, each one a path into the unknown.

Dog sleds or hot-air balloons, provisions, and the decision of what team to accompany you into the wilderness; each choice represents a lifeline, a delicate balance between speed, safety and the unknown perils of the journey ahead.

Brave souls will follow your lead, their lives entrusted to your planning and decision making. The thrill of being the first to conquer the North Pole is intoxicating, a siren's call that drowns out the whispers of caution. Yet, the spectre of the unknown casts a long shadow over your ambition.

You imagine the challenges that lie ahead. The crunch of snow underfoot, the howling winds that threaten to steer you off course, the treacherous ice ridges that rise like monstrous waves. Will the dog sleds be able to navigate the unpredictable terrain? Will the hot-air balloon withstand the ferocious Arctic storms?

Fear and doubt creep into your mind, their icy tendrils attempting to grasp your resolve. But your ambition burns brighter, a flame that refuses to be extinguished. You are driven, perhaps beyond reason, by the promise of glory, the allure of the unknown, the desire to etch your name into the annals of history.

With a deep breath, you steel yourself against the onslaught of your fears. The journey is fraught with danger, the path unclear, but the call of the North Pole is irresistible. You are committed, ready to step into the unknown.

Now, imagine yourself as a member of a management team, standing on the precipice of a Strategic Initiative like Automation. You're back in the safety of the boardroom, but the feeling is quite similar. The goal is clear – to automate processes and increase efficiency. But the path to get there, the challenges you will face, and the resources you will need are all uncertain.

Just as the polar explorer had to choose between dog sleds and hot-air balloons, you now have to decide what tools and tactics will best serve your initiative. Will you automate production processes or administrative tasks? Will you face resistance from employees or technical hurdles? Will your existing resources suffice, or will you need new software, training, or perhaps a complete overhaul of your IT infrastructure?

The weight of responsibility is heavy. Your decisions will affect not just the success of the initiative, but the livelihoods of your employees and the future of your organization. The allure of being the first in your industry to fully automate, of gaining a competitive edge, is tantalizing. But the path to that glory is uncertain, with plenty of potential pitfalls.

And just as the polar explorer learned, venturing into the unknown without a clear plan is dangerous. Many expeditions failed, not because of courage or determination, but because they were ill-prepared for the challenges they encountered. They set out too hastily, without fully understanding the perils of the journey.

Similarly, as a member of the management team, rushing to implement a Strategic Initiative without fully appreciating its implications can lead to failure. A compelling vision and a well-crafted presentation are not sufficient. Understanding the specifics – the processes, potential obstacles and required resources – is crucial. Without this clarity, the initiative could become aimless.

This overconfidence, while driving ambition, can also create organizational confusion. Overestimating clarity and capabilities often results in a disconnect between ambition and actual execution. This is a common trap, leading to slow adoption and failure in strategy execution.

Unlike early explorers, today's leaders have access to the necessary tools and knowledge. The real challenge lies in recognizing the importance of thorough planning and resisting the urge to act prematurely. Just as successful expeditions require meticulous preparation and an understanding of challenges, so too does a successful Strategic Initiative.

THE STRATEGIC ASSESSMENT™

Strategy execution is a complex process that requires a full understanding of an organization's capabilities, as well as the potential obstacles it might face.

Each company has distinct characteristics, shaped by its history, culture and past experiences. These characteristics define its unique strengths and areas of vulnerability. In my decade-long journey in strategic implementation, I've observed that while the foundational principles of strategy are consistent, the specifics of execution vary significantly from one organization to another.

With this insight, my team and I dedicated ourselves to uncovering the underlying factors that determine successful strategy execution. Our objective was to identify the essential variables that significantly impact an organization's strategic outcomes and to distinguish them from factors that might *seem* important but have minimal impact. After an intensive two-year research period, we developed a predictive model capable of assessing a company's likelihood of strategic success. This model not only provides a diagnostic overview but also offers recommendations for areas of improvement and actionable steps for leadership.

We named this tool Assessment. It's not a standard evaluation tool; Assessment is a refined system that emphasizes the most critical aspects of strategic success. It is designed to be a valuable resource for consultants, enabling them to engage effectively with an organization's top leadership. The goal of Assessment is to ensure that the strategies developed are not only robust in theory but are also well-equipped for practical implementation and success.

For a CEO, achieving success in these areas is not only the primary duty of the role; it is also the path to creating lasting structural capital within the company that secures success for future strategies. The competencies assessed by our tool are directly linked with increased growth, profitability and shareholder value, setting the top leaders apart from the rest.

While the primary focus of this book is on a specific method for strategy execution – encompassing a distinct thought process, breaking down goals into actionable steps, rigorous prioritization, and emphasizing effective communication – it's essential to recognize that strategy execution's real-world performance is influenced by various other factors.

The Assessment tool addresses these factors. Before we delve into crafting MIGs, Strategic Initiatives and Key Activities, we make sure that the strategic foundation is solid. After all, building on unstable ground can jeopardize an entire structure.

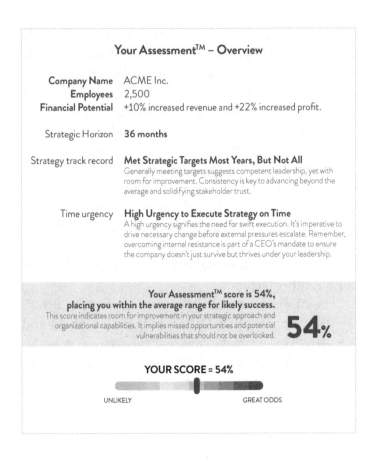

I've identified six critical areas that significantly impact successful strategy execution, beyond the methodology discussed in this book:

1. **Strategic Clarity & Priority**

   This perspective evaluates the CEO's ability to formulate and communicate a clear strategy. It focuses on how well the strategy is understood and embraced by the management team and assesses their ability to prioritize effectively within the strategic framework. We're looking for a clear direction that's compelling and concentrated on critical priorities.

2. Ability to Change

This dimension measures the organization's adaptability and responsiveness to change. It explores how effectively the leadership can motivate and lead the organization through transformation, its ability to maintain momentum during change, and the commitment to embed lasting improvements. The intent is to foster an environment where change is embraced and executed efficiently.

3. Leadership

The Leadership dimension evaluates the quality and effectiveness of leadership throughout the organization. It assesses leaders' ability to drive and implement strategy, their urgency in responding to change, and their ability to foster accountability and performance culture. The focus is on cultivating strong, aligned leadership that propels the organization toward its goals.

4. Goal Structure

This area looks at how the organization breaks down its strategic goals into actionable, measurable plans. It examines the alignment and coherence of these plans across different levels of the organization, ensuring that strategies are not only well-articulated but also effectively translated into departmental actions and individual responsibilities.

5. Measurability

Measurability focuses on the organization's ability to track and measure progress toward its strategic goals. It assesses the systems and processes in place for monitoring performance and how well these indicators are communicated and understood across the organization. It's about creating a performance-focused culture where progress is measured, understood and acted upon.

6. **C-suite Conditions**

This dimension is specifically concerned with the CEO's personal effectiveness in leading the organization's strategy. It assesses the CEO's allocation of time to strategic tasks, the clarity and quality of information available for making strategic decisions, and the CEO's overall satisfaction with strategic execution. It's about ensuring that the top leadership is well-equipped, informed and actively engaged.

The methodology outlined in this book and the Assessment are intrinsically linked. While the methodology provides a comprehensive road map for strategy, the Assessment fortifies this approach, ensuring that organizations set out on their strategic journey from a position of strength. Together, they optimize the likelihood of successful execution, creating a synergistic approach to strategy.

INSIGHTS FROM ASSESSMENT

Over the past two years, my team and I have conducted more than 300 Assessments across a diverse range of companies. These companies varied greatly in size, industry and maturity, yet we found they had plenty in common.

Based on these Assessments, we built a comprehensive study, a blend of qualitative and quantitative analysis. Imagine it as a series of in-depth interviews with CEOs and their top team members. Each interview gave us a unique story, but when we put them all together, we got a clear picture of how businesses today are trying to carry out their strategies.

Let's explore some of the key insights we unearthed.

It was found that 85% of CEOs strongly agreed with the statement: "I have a clearly defined strategy." On the surface, this might suggest a high degree of strategic clarity. However, when we dug deeper, we found a different story. Their own management teams were ambiguous about the clarity in the strategy, and especially about the agreement within the priorities. This suggests a significant disconnect between the CEO's perception and the team's reality. This insight from our own data is echoed by the previously cited MIT article titled "No One Knows Your Strategy," which revealed that only about 51% of the average management team agrees on the priorities within a strategy.

To bridge this chasm, I looked for a clear way to measure strategic clarity. I found that focusing on Strategic Initiatives, which outline how goals will be achieved, was the answer. By checking how much of a company's growth is covered by these initiatives, we get a clear picture of strategic quality. Simply put, if top leaders can pinpoint where growth will come from, the strategy is clearer. However, our Assessment data showed that companies could only account for 32% of their planned growth. This shows that many overestimate how clear their strategy really is.

Only 53% of CEOs are happy with how their management teams focus on key areas. While these managers are good at handling daily tasks and improving their operational scorecards, they often stumble when it comes to making the big strategic changes needed for future success. This challenge is made even harder by a general reluctance to change and a sense of compla-cency, leading companies to stick to what they know.

The root of the issue might well be the unclear strategy. If the strategy isn't clear, how can managers prioritize effectively? The dissatisfaction CEOs feel toward their teams might actually reflect back on their own overconfidence and reluctance to acknowledge where the real problem lies. Instead of seeing the lack of urgency as the main issue, it might just be a sign of a deeper problem: an unclear strategy.

The importance of aligning time and effort with strategic priorities is underscored by a study on "Man-aging Initiative Overload," by Bain & Company.[3] The study revealed a startling imbalance:

"80% of a leader's time is allocated to priorities that account for less than 20% of the company's value."

This finding highlights the critical need for leaders to reassess and realign their priorities so that their efforts are directed toward initiatives that truly drive value for the company.

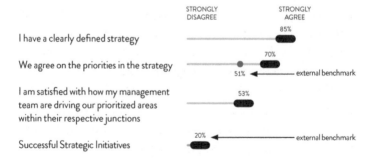

The insights we've shared culminate in a sobering conclusion, one that is not unique to our study but is echoed in many other research pieces and is a well-documented observation in the field of strategic management: **only 20% of Strategic Initiatives deliver their intended financial impact on time.**[7] This statistic, while daunting, underscores the critical importance of strategic clarity, unity and effective execution in achieving business success.

As a side note, if you, as a CEO, are considering conducting a strategic assessment for your company, please feel free to reach out using the contact details provided at the end of this book. The Assessment is free of charge as part of our research investment. Please note that it is available only to CEOs of companies with 500 or more employees, in line with our study's scope and objectives.

OWNERSHIP, SELF-AWARENESS AND COMMUNICATION

Navigating the complex terrain of strategic execution requires a keen understanding of three pivotal insights. These insights, gleaned from years of experience and countless assessments, are the guiding principles that illuminate the path to success.

Firstly, as leaders, you are the custodians of your company's strategic direction. The level of clarity and precision you bring to this role directly influences the outcomes. It's a straightforward equation: vague direction leads to vague results. Owning the strategy is crucial. You must be clear, concise and personally invested in your Strategic Initiatives.

The essence of the matter extends beyond merely accepting the role of a strategic custodian. The real test of ownership comes in how you prioritize your time and attention. It's not enough to simply set the strategy and expect others to carry it out. You need to be actively involved, leading by example, demonstrating through your actions that the strategy really matters. This means dedicating your time, being present and engaged, and standing shoulder-to-shoulder with your team as you navigate the path toward your goals.

Secondly, the pitfall of self-overestimation is a common stumbling block among leaders. It's easy to assume that your strategic vision is crystal clear when you're the one who's spent countless hours crafting it. However, this clarity might not translate to your team as effectively as you think. This is where the importance of self-awareness comes into play. It's not enough to simply communicate your strategy; you must also be aware of how it's being perceived and understood. This means being open to feedback, willing to adjust your communication style, and acknowledging that what seems clear to you may be a foggy concept to others. It's about bridging the gap between your understanding and your team's perception.

Lastly, let's consider the vital role of communication. Without clear, consistent and effective communication, your strategy risks remaining an abstract concept, disconnected from the day-to-day operations of your organization.

However, communication is often overlooked or treated as a one-off event. The reality is that it's an ongoing process, requiring continuous effort and attention. It's not just about delivering a polished PowerPoint presentation filled with buzzwords and then considering the job done.

We're now going to tie these three insights together and look at a crucial aspect of strategic execution:

defining sub-initiatives. This is where the rubber meets the road, where MIGs and Strategic Initiatives are transformed into actionable steps, and where the abstract becomes concrete.

AWAKENING TO A NEW DAWN

A sense of anticipation tingled in Fiona's veins, an echo of the previous day's strategic discussions. With the first light of dawn as her companion, she embarked on a brisk jog, her heart pounding in rhythm with the promise of the day ahead.

When she returned, the rest of the management team was already gathered for breakfast. The air was charged with a current of shared purpose, a stark contrast to the weary resignation of yesterday. It was as if they were standing on the precipice of something transformative, their collective energy humming with potential. Their breakfast chatter was a symphony of optimism.

They went up to the meeting room, remembering yesterday's intense deliberations.

The CEO stood up, his presence filling the room. His words of appreciation for the team's dedication and the shared enjoyment of the previous evening's dinner echoed warmly in the room. Then, with a determined air, he directed their focus toward the day's agenda.

"Today," the CEO began, "we're going to take our Strategic Initiatives and shape them into something that we can confidently present to our board and, more importantly, to our staff. Let's consider our Automation initiative. What does it mean in practical terms? It could mean a multitude of things, especially for those who weren't part of yesterday's discussions. Our task today is to continue refining and prioritizing within each of our chosen Strategic Initiatives.

"We've received a wealth of ideas and suggestions from the organization, which is testament to the engagement of our teams. But, as we acknowledged yesterday, there are always more good ideas than there is capacity to execute. The sheer volume of suggestions is encouraging, but to identify what really matters, we'll have to say no to most of them. As Steve Jobs once said, 'Innovation is saying no to a thousand things.'

"We shouldn't shy away from potential reactions at this stage. I firmly believe that nothing boosts morale more than winning, and that's precisely why we're here to set the stage."

"Nothing is more counterintuitive for a leader than saying no to a good idea, and nothing is a bigger destroyer of focus than always saying yes. I have found nothing that drives the morale and engagement of a team more than winning."

– JIM HULING

Jim Huling's career, spanning corporate leadership roles in Fortune 500 companies and as a CEO of an award-winning organization, positions him as a champion of strategic decision making. Jim's practical insights, shared through his syndicated column 'The Business of Life,' offer valuable guidance on balancing a thriving career with a fulfilling personal life.

SUB-INITIATIVES

Sub-initiatives are concrete, actionable projects that bring a Strategic Initiative to life. They are tangible steps that translate the broader strategy into specific actions.

Consider our Automation initiative. A potential sub-initiative could be the implementation of a Customer Service Chatbot, designed to automate the repetitive task of answering common customer queries. This project is a specific, measurable movement that directly contributes to the broader Automation initiative.

Sub-initiatives usually have a shorter lifespan than their parent Strategic Initiatives, often completed within 6 to 12 months. This immediacy makes them more relatable and manageable for the teams charged with their execution.

The principle of prioritization is equally crucial when deciding which sub-initiatives to pursue. It's about identifying the most impactful levers to pull. Not all sub-initiatives will have the same impact, so it's essential to focus on those that will drive the most significant progress toward the Strategic Initiative and, ultimately, the MIGs.

It's common to have a surplus of ideas when it comes to sub-initiatives, most of them bubbling up from the organization. The challenge lies in not letting the good stand in the way of the great. By funnelling resources to where they matter the most and sifting through the myriad of possibilities, you'll find the gold nuggets that will really make a difference.

REVISITING THE PURPOSE

Fiona revisited the PowerPoint slide from yesterday's meeting, outlining the Strategic Initiatives. Alex said, "This is a great start. It's clear, but we need to understand more about the impact of automation."

Richard, the CFO, was not convinced. "Yes, but it doesn't really say much, does it? If I were to present this to my team, they'd probably dismiss it as management jargon. We need to be more concrete. Isn't that what we're supposed to do today?" He turned to the CEO, seeking confirmation.

The CEO, acknowledging the need for practicality, responded, "Let's take these ideas from the organization and focus on the most impactful. We're looking for game-changing automation projects that significantly affect our bottom line without excessive costs."

He gestured toward the list of concrete project ideas, "These range from automated time reporting to full warehouse automation. We need to identify which of these will truly drive our strategy forward and make a meaningful difference to our operations."

They reviewed all the sub-initiatives, rating them based on economic impact and investment requirements. The list of around 40 ideas was whittled down to a more manageable five. A distinct trio emerged that could be implemented in parallel, requiring minimal overlapping resources and offering substantial potential upside.

"The first sub-initiative," the CEO began, "is Warehouse Pick-and-Pack Automation. We aim to streamline our warehouse operations, reducing the time it takes to fulfill orders and, therefore, minimizing errors. This will not only improve our service quality but hugely increase productivity, while at the same time reducing costs associated with mis-picks and returns."

He moved on to the second sub-initiative. "The implementation of a Customer Service Chatbot. By automating responses to common customer queries, we can provide faster, round-the-clock support. This will enhance customer satisfaction and free up our customer service team to handle more complex issues, also greatly improving the productivity of that department within the operations leg of the company; a big cost driver."

"Lastly," he concluded, "we will automate our Sales Process. By using technology to manage routine tasks, our sales team can focus on building relationships and closing deals. This will increase our sales efficiency and effectiveness, contributing directly to our profit margins. Among other things, the tech would automate Lead Qualification in CRM, automate the quote-process, and automate email and follow-up sequences."

STRATEGIC INITIATIVES
AUTOMATION

Sub-initiatives

Warehouse Pick-and-Pack
Upgrade WMS, Barcode Scanning & RFID, WMS to ERP integration, Automated Conveyer Sorting

Customer Service Chatbot
Select and deploy NLP-bot, Train on common queries, Implement escalation rules

Sales Process Automation
Automate Lead Qualification in CRM, Automate Quote-process, automated email and follow-up sequences

When they broke for lunch, they had crafted a clear road map. It pinpointed their MIGs, each with a distinct starting line, finish line and deadline. To achieve these goals, they had identified five Strategic Initiatives, each with a clear purpose.

MOST IMPORTANT GOALS	**Increase Revenue** from 1,200 million to 2,050 million *Due in 36 months*	**Increase Profit** from 40 million (3.3%) to 160 million (7.8%) *Due in 36 months*

STRATEGIC INITIATIVES
Sub-initiatives

Expansion
• Key Account Program
• Value Based Pricing Initiative
• Large Account Business Development

Automation
• Warehouse Pick-and-Pack
• Customer Service Chatbot
• Sales Process Automation

Merger
• Strategic Synergies & Operational Efficiency Program
• Cross Selling Opportunities
• Cultural Integration
• Customer Retention

Cost Savings Initiative
• Fixed Cost Reduction Program
• Focus Loss Making Units

UK Launch
• Hire & Legal
• Go to Market
• Sales & Partners

The layer of sub-initiatives provided further clarity, detailing the meaning of each initiative, and outlining who was expected to contribute. The only remaining task was to communicate this strategy effectively. But before we explore that, let's turn our attention to the next part: Execution.

PART II

EXECUTION

As we move from planning to doing, we recognize that understanding our goals was just the beginning. The real drama unfolds in the trenches, where strategy meets the test of reality, where lofty aspirations come face-to-face with real-world challenges.

Navigating the complexities of execution is like walking a tightrope. On one side, there's the risk of inertia, where initiatives languish and eventually wither away, stifled by bureaucracy and a resistance to change. On the other side, there's the peril of aimless activity, a flurry of efforts that lack focus and direction, leading to wasted resources and lost opportunities.

The stakes are huge. A lapse in execution can trigger a domino effect of setbacks – demoralized teams, squandered resources and a strategy that remains confined to PowerPoint slides. It's a scenario where accountability becomes elusive, where meetings are many, but milestones are few. It's where the committed grow disillusioned, eventually seeking environments where their passion is reciprocated.

But this is more than a cautionary tale. It's a clarion call. We must recognize the urgency that our volatile, uncertain world imposes upon us. There's a need for precision and agility in our actions, for a new breed of leadership that combines vision with the ability to execute.

So, prepare yourself for an immersive journey into the art and science of making things happen. So, prepare yourself for an immersive journey into the art and science of making things happen. We're about to explore the mechanics of turning strategic visions into tangible results, of transforming the 'what' and 'why' into the 'how.' It's here that the Execution Revolution truly shines, forging legacies in the foundry of action.

CHAPTER 4

KEY ACTIVITIES AND THE DIFFERENCE BETWEEN INPUTS AND OUTCOMES

"A goal without a plan is just a wish."

– ANTOINE DE SAINT-EXUPÉRY

Antoine de Saint-Exupéry was a revered figure in French literature and aviation. Widely recognized for his classic novella *Le Petit Prince* (The Little Prince), de Saint-Exupéry's profound insights into purposeful action and determination continue to inspire readers around the world.

When we set out to achieve our goals, whether in our personal lives or professional domains, we often find ourselves navigating the interplay between inputs and outcomes. Outcomes are the tangible results that keep us up at night – the turnover, the profit, or in a more everyday context, our weight. These are the end results we can see and measure, but they are often the product of less visible factors – the inputs.

While it's essential to measure outcomes to understand our current performance, relying solely on them can be misleading. Think of outcomes as the view from a car's rear-view mirror. They show us the path we've travelled, but they don't give us a clear picture of the road ahead. The actions that resulted in these outcomes might have taken place 3-6 months ago, or even longer. So, when we base our decisions only on these outcomes, we're essentially navigating our company using outdated information.

Just as constantly checking our weight on a set of scales won't lead to weight loss, obsessing over past outcomes won't propel us toward our future goals. We need to look ahead, anticipate challenges and make proactive decisions. Steering a company by only focusing on past outcomes is like driving while solely looking in the rear-view mirror. We need to be proactive, not reactive.

KEY ACTIVITIES

The real key to achieving our goals isn't just about focusing on the end result, but honing in on the actions – the critical activities that push our goals forward. Think again about the weight loss example. The real game-changers are diet and exercise. These are the things we can control, and they're what will determine whether we succeed or not. This isn't a complex concept, but it's a crucial one: focusing on our actions is the most effective way to influence our results.

However, it's easy to get caught up in the end result. This often happens because it's easier to measure, and it's ultimately what we're aiming for. But once we understand the importance of identifying and measuring the right actions, it becomes a natural part of our process.

We refer to these actions as **Key Activities**, because they're the ones that have the biggest impact. The principle here is that a small number of activities will drive most of our results. Therefore, it's essential to identify these high-impact activities and focus our efforts there, rather than trying to measure everything we do. By building an organizational model that optimizes and rewards these Key Activities, we set ourselves up for success.

CAVEMEN IN THE WORKPLACE

Let's now consider the three characteristics that make Key Activities truly impactful. To do this, we need to acknowledge that beneath the surface of our modern lives, our brains haven't changed much since prehistoric days and, as a result, we often fall into behavioural traps that don't serve us well in the modern world.

THE REACTIVITY TRAP

First and foremost, we're hardwired to react. Our amygdala, the primal part of our brain, manages fight or flight, helping to keep us safe. But in a work environment, this instinctive reactivity can be both stressful and inefficient. The modern office is a minefield of potential distractions: urgent emails, pop-up notifications, impending meetings, looming deadlines. And our brains can't get enough of it. Even when we've planned to tackle something far more important, these reactive tasks have a knack for elbowing their way to the front of the line.

This constant reactivity can quickly consume any proactive ambitions we might have. We've all experienced it: on Sunday, we earmark a few truly proactive tasks as our objectives for the week. These are the tasks that would add an extra layer of value compared to the usual rhythm of business-as-usual weeks. But then Monday rolls around, and before we know it, we're swept up in a whirlwind of ad-hoc meetings and email replies. Suddenly, those proactive tasks we were so keen on are pushed to the back burner, relegated as "next week's problem." And the cycle continues.

The first hallmark of high-impact Key Activities is proactivity. By consciously focusing on proactive behaviours, we can help our caveman brains overcome their reactive tendencies. And this allows us to create opportunities that wouldn't exist if we just sat back and waited.

THE URGENCY BIAS

Our second pitfall is the tendency of our brains to prioritize what's urgent over what's important. However, those who excel in their fields understand that to really make a difference, you need to focus on what's important today to secure a better tomorrow. This forms the second characteristic of a high-impact Key Activity.

"The real enemy of execution is your day job!"

– STEPHEN COVEY

This often stems from our human struggle with delayed gratification. We find it challenging to commit to activities whose payoff is in the distant future, while tasks with immediate rewards are far more enticing. In the everyday workplace, meeting the deadline of an urgent task provides an immediate sense of accomplishment, and we naturally gravitate toward such tasks.

The tricky part is that proactive behaviours don't naturally come with deadlines, and the cost of reactivity becomes apparent over time. It's only when winter arrives that we realize we should've built a shelter and stockpiled food. Similarly, in the workplace, putting off important but long-term tasks might not seem like a big deal in the short term. But eventually, it becomes clear who's thriving and who's just surviving.

So, when designing Key Activities, focus your efforts on tasks that matter, rather than getting lost in the whirlwind of your daily routine. This is your chance to outsmart your inner caveman brain and steer it toward areas that need a little nudge. Turn your natural tendencies into your superpowers and use them to propel you forward.

THE COMFORT ZONE
Thirdly, we have a natural tendency to stick to what we know, to stay within our comfort zones. This is our amygdala at work, preferring the familiar and the safe. We're drawn to tasks and activities that we're already good at. It's human nature. But deep down, we all know that real growth and high performance come from stepping out of that comfort zone and taking on new challenges.

"It is not because things are difficult that we do not dare; it is because we do not dare that things are difficult."

– SENECA

Seneca, a Stoic philosopher, highlights the transformative power of courage and personal responsibility in shaping life's experiences.

This is true in many aspects of life, including business. Consider the competitive edge you could gain by mastering tactics that your competitors haven't yet grasped. For instance, while everyone else is cold calling lower-level stakeholders and making small, price-pressured deals, you could be reaching out to higher-level contacts, accessing larger budgets, and securing more significant deals.

That's why the third characteristic of impactful Key Activities is to seek out tasks that are a bit challenging. Perhaps you've attempted them before and stumbled, or maybe you haven't been able to maintain a high enough volume for them to make a difference. But imagine the competitive advantage your team could gain by consistently performing these challenging tasks. You'd leave your competitors in the dust. So, when designing your Key Activities, don't shy away from the hard stuff. Embrace it, because it's where real growth happens.

Proactive
not reactive

Important
not urgent

Challenging
not comfortable

Key Activities
Has a direct effect to the lag measure and steering &
measuring it affect its frequency, quality or outcome.

Low-Impact Activities
Steering & measuring it doesn't affect its frequency,
quality or outcome.

STEPPING OUT OF THE CAVE

When we combine the three principles of proactive, important and challenging tasks, we create a trifecta that can be quite uncomfortable for us to process. These tasks, despite their potential to significantly impact our goals, can trigger our old nemesis: procrastination. Suddenly, that overdue report from last week seems appealing, or we convince ourselves that we need to do more research before embarking on our task. We're drawn to these more comfortable tasks like a moth to a light, seeking the security they offer.

We find ourselves overthinking, creating a narrative that the task at hand is more complex than it really is, or that we're not equipped to tackle it. We might tell ourselves, "I need to do more research," or "I need more practice," or even, "I'll start tomorrow."

These hurdles we perceive aren't insurmountable barriers; they're merely shadows of reluctance, the echoes of comfort zones that have kept us anchored in the familiar. But greatness isn't birthed from the cradle of convenience. It's forged in the fires of the bold resolve to embrace the novel and the challenging.

Acknowledging this resistance as a natural reaction to the uncharted and the new is the first stride in the march of the Execution Revolution. With this recognition, we can consciously choose to advance, knowing that in this realm, growth and excellence are born.

Designing your Key Activities isn't about adding complexity; it's about simplicity, intentionality and significance. It's about seizing the gauntlet that the Execution Revolution throws down before us – choosing to engage, not evade; to charge ahead, not retreat.

83

TEAM WORKSHOP

A week had passed since Alex, the Chief Sales & Marketing Officer, and the company management team had hammered out the company's MIGs and Strategic Initiatives. Today was the day he'd been gearing up for, the day he would rally his troops and set them on a new path. His Sales & Marketing department was a diverse group, spread across two continents, with over 300 employees.

Alex was a man of action, and he knew that today's meeting would set the pace for the coming months. This was a significant shift in strategy, and he understood that some of his team might be resistant to change. But Alex was not one to back down from a challenge.

PREPARATIONS

Knowing the influence they held within the team, he had taken the time to brief his two most trusted lieutenants: Elinor, their head of US Field Sales, and Jessica, her EU and APAC counterpart. He had explicitly asked for their support, explaining that this new approach was a directive from the CEO and that Alex himself saw this as a golden opportunity.

His team was primarily responsible for driving the revenue side of their MIGs, but he knew there were also things they could do to improve the margins on the deals they were making.

As his team logged into their virtual meeting, Alex could feel his adrenaline pumping. "Today, we're setting off on a journey that I believe will take this company, and especially us in sales and marketing, to new heights. We've decided to bring more focus to our work, and I see this as a game-changer for us. So, let's get down to business."

THE RULES OF THE GAME

"Let's kick things off by understanding our playing field and getting familiar with the rules of the game. This year, we're honing in on what truly matters. We're not trying to juggle a dozen balls at once; instead, we're focusing on the two that will make the biggest impact. These are our MIGs, the ones that will get our utmost attention and effort.

"In addition to these goals, we've identified a few Strategic Initiatives. These are the tactics we believe will bridge the gap between where we are now and where we want to be. They're our road map to achieving our MIGs.

"Today, our task is to figure out how we, as a function, can contribute to this journey. We're not just spectators; we're players in this game. But, as we all know, we've fallen short of our targets over the past three years, despite our growth. But that's in the past. Today, we're looking forward, and we're ready to hit our targets head-on.

"'Less is more' has been the approach taken by our CEO, and I expect us to echo his sentiment. We need to generate $850 million in new sales over the next three years." He made sure to not pause after this statement since he knew that number was ambitious, to say the least. "The good news is that there are a couple of initiatives that will help us greatly along the way. And each initiative will not only have our full focus but also from the CEO and the whole organization. We are not alone, and we will succeed, I'm sure of it."

ANCHORING HIS TEAMS' CONTRIBUTION

"First up, I'm thrilled to announce that we're moving forward with the acquisition many of you have been eagerly anticipating. This isn't just about the immediate financial gain of $140 million – it also opens up a whole new world of opportunities for us. We're looking at nearly 400 potential clients ripe for upselling and cross-selling. And the best part? Almost all of them represent uncharted territory. We're not treading on familiar ground here; we're looking at shiny, new revenue opportunities." Alex paused, hoping for some backup from his two most vocal deputies. Right on cue, Elinor chimed in.

"Apologies for interrupting, Alex, but I just have to say, this is fantastic news!" Elinor's enthusiasm was infectious. "My team had a chance to look into their client list during the due diligence process, and let me tell you, it's a goldmine. The client type aligns perfectly with our segmentation strategy, and there's massive potential for doubling them when we add our product offerings. Sure, it'll take some fancy strategic sales manoeuvres to make it happen, but if you keep bringing us news like this, Alex, I'm all in."

Alex made a mental note to thank Elinor later. He knew she relished being in the know before others, and he could always count on her support in return. But for now, he had to keep the momentum going. "Thanks, Elinor. I've heard similar things, and we'll delve deeper into those strategic manoeuvres you mentioned later this afternoon. But for now, let's move on."

Alex, with his characteristic energy, continued to lay out the MIGs. He emphasized the need to strike a balance between driving revenue and improving margins. He took the time to explain the rationale behind each decision made by the management team, ensuring that everyone on his team understood and felt invested in the process. He also detailed the company's Strategic Initiatives and how they were expected to contribute.

LEAD THE CHANGE

In a world where change is the only constant, being a catalyst for change isn't just the better choice – it's the only choice. Consider the rest of your career and the disruptions that still lie ahead. The speed of change is forever increasing, so mastering the skills of driving change will be a crucial hallmark for successful leaders of the future.

In certain situations, like the one you're facing now, it's wise to do some smart pre-work. Engage the strongest voices on your team in advance and explicitly ask for their support. Focus on the 'why' of the message to ensure that you gain their support not by force but by voluntary enrollment. This approach will not only strengthen your team's commitment, but will also pave the way for a smoother transition.

The power to steer your team toward success or failure rests squarely on your shoulders. Take a moment, gather your thoughts and make your decision. Remember, you're not just a manager, you're a leader – the catalyst for positive change.

CHANGES AHEAD

The initiative that would have the most significant impact on their everyday processes was the drive to upsell and cross-sell their offerings within the Expansion Initiative. This was crucial for the success of their merger, and also a process they would need going forward. The reality was that they had over 2,500 clients, but each client typically only purchased one or two of their five product offerings. There was immense potential for the top 200 clients to buy the full suite, and for the top 1,000 to buy from at least one more business line.

The current setup incentivized each salesperson only on their specific product line, creating a sense of distrust when bringing other business lines into the sales conversation. This fear of complicating the deal with more stakeholders often held them back. As a result, they were not leveraging their extensive client base effectively and were operating like five separate sales organizations with no clear strategy for Key Account Management.

Fortunately, the third initiative they were tackling was a significant upgrade to their CRM system, within the Automation Initiative. This would not only automate tasks such as lead generation and sales follow-ups but also provide an opportunity to significantly improve their cross-selling process. There was also the potential for upselling from customer operations to consider, which would boost their numbers nicely.

Lastly, specifically for their European organization, there was the UK Launch. Since Brexit, they had not had any staff to cover that area, but it was time to get moving again. The UK had been a profitable market for them in the past, and now his management team had the task of re-establishing their UK presence.

As Alex wrapped up his introduction, he felt a sense of accomplishment. It was rare to present something so concrete to the group. Almost half of the team had raised their virtual hands, eager to ask questions or share their thoughts. Alex knew the importance of these initial reactions and how they could sway the group's overall sentiment.

OPENING UP

Even though Elinor had already expressed her excitement, Alex decided to shift his attention to Jessica, the other manager he had briefed earlier. Jessica oversaw almost one third of his entire organization and her reaction was crucial, given the significant changes her team would have to undergo.

He had given Jessica a few days to digest the information, but he knew she had a challenging journey ahead. Alex was concerned that the top-down nature of the decision might make Jessica feel sidelined. However, as he had hoped, Jessica voiced her support.

"I know this is a big shift for us," Jessica began. "It's going to be a challenge, no doubt about it. But I also see the potential here. The potential for growth, for improvement, and for really making a difference. So, I'm on board, Alex. We're on board. Let's do this."

Alex felt a surge of relief. Jessica's endorsement, her willingness to embrace the challenge, was exactly the response he had hoped for. He also understood that her hesitation was natural, given the magnitude of the changes. But he was confident that with time, she would see the benefits and fully embrace the new direction.

Alex was already planning his next steps, thinking about how to support Jessica and the rest of his team through this transition. He knew there would be challenges ahead, but he was ready to face them head-on. After all, that's what leaders do.

> *"A leader is one who knows the way,*
> *goes the way, and shows the way."*
>
> **– JOHN C. MAXWELL**

John C. Maxwell, a prolific author and renowned leadership expert, is celebrated for his impactful contributions to the fields of leadership and personal development. With over 100 books and numerous articles, including being a #1 *New York Times* bestselling author, Maxwell is a trusted guide for individuals and organizations seeking to enhance their leadership skills.

STEP BY STEP

As a team leader, you hold the baton passed down from the higher ranks of your organization, and you also have the power to shape your team's future. Your mission, should you choose to accept it, is twofold: to secure your team's buy-in and to define their contribution. And yes, the order matters.

You understand your team's strengths, weaknesses, hopes and fears. But if you're feeling a bit uncertain about this part of the journey, rest assured that you're not alone. Over the years, I've gleaned some tried-and-true best practices from truly great leaders, having had the benefit of working with hundreds of teams in similar situations. But first, let's focus on the elephant in the room.

Your team members also know you. They can read your emotions, too, so if you enter the room shrouded in a cloud of doubt, they'll sense it. If you're wrestling with your own resistance to change, they'll see it. And if you're already crafting your defeat speech, they'll hear it. The message will be loud and clear: "Our leader doesn't believe we can do this."

"Confidence is contagious;
so is lack of confidence."

– VINCE LOMBARDI

Vince Lombardi, celebrated as a legendary figure in American football coaching, achieved remarkable success by leading the Green Bay Packers to five NFL championships.

Change is a challenge, even under the best circumstances. As a leader, you're often caught in a unique predicament, trying to personally adapt to change while simultaneously driving it within your organization. It's a delicate balancing act, and it's tough to manage the latter when you're still grappling with the former.

But here's the thing: once the company has charted its course and the time for debate has passed, you face a critical choice. Will you be a force for change, propelling your team forward, or will you be a dragging anchor of the status quo, holding them back?

The cost of failing to secure buy-in is steep. It leads to delays at every stage of the change journey. In an external environment that demands constant change at 21st-century speed, this organizational incapacity can relegate some companies to the sidelines.

"Nothing is constant but change."

– HERACLITUS

Heraclitus, the eminent ancient Greek philosopher, made profound contributions to metaphysics and our understanding of reality. His insights on the ever-evolving universe and the fluidity of existence continue to influence philosophical thought and inspire contemplation on the dynamic nature of life and reality.

DEFINING YOUR CONTRIBUTION

As a leader, your next task, once you've secured your team's buy-in, is to guide their focus. This involves a few crucial steps, so let's break them down.

Teams often struggle to differentiate between goals (outputs) and activities (inputs), which can cloud their focus. Your first mission is to spotlight outputs

– the goals your team can directly influence and that align with the overarching objectives from above.

Consider the following: if the company's primary objective is profitability, a customer support department might focus on enhancing productivity. This approach directs the team's attention toward improving processes, and incentivizes behaviours that ultimately save the company money and increase profits. On the other hand, if the company is aiming for revenue growth, the same support department could zero in on reducing customer churn. This demonstrates that their contribution might not be in generating new sales, but in ensuring that once customers enter, they stay.

It's vital that your team can fully own their goal. This means it should be something they can directly influence, rather than being overly dependent on the contributions of other teams.

"Individual commitment to a group effort
– that is what makes a team work, a company
work, a society work, a civilization work."

– VINCE LOMBARDI

A productive way to approach this is to initiate a brainstorming session. At this stage, all ideas are welcome, as long as they align with the overarching goals. Encourage your team to suggest ideas, as this fosters a sense of ownership, a concept developed by Edwin Locke in the mid-20th century. The principle is simple: employees are more committed to goals they've had a hand in setting.

Once you've gathered all the ideas, it's time for a quick round of separating goals from activities. Many of the suggestions will likely be inputs, which are valuable but more relevant for later stages. After refining the list down to outputs and merging similar ideas, you'll typically end up with 5-15 potential goals.

The next step is to apply the principle of focusing on less to achieve more. A straightforward way to do this is to hold a vote. Give each team member two votes – one for what they believe is the most impactful goal, and another for the second most impactful. This process often leads to a consensus on what matters the most, while also highlighting that other options are less important.

As a leader, your primary responsibility is to ensure alignment from your team toward the direction coming from above. If there's resistance to the new direction and a tendency to cling to the old ways, it's your role to gently steer the conversation back on track. Some ideas might seem excellent in isolation, but they may not align with the new strategic focus.

While it's important to foster team engagement and not just dictate the course, there are times when a leader's veto is necessary. This veto should only be exercised when the group consensus diverges from the company's direction. Interestingly, experience shows that invoking a veto often sparks a positive discussion within the team, further clarifying the task at hand.

However, with the power of veto comes the responsibility of explanation. If you use your veto, you must clarify why. Remind your team of their mission: to identify what they can focus on that supports the overarching goals. You're not an island; you're part of a larger entity, and your contribution to the whole is crucial.

As you move forward, keep in mind two guiding principles that can greatly enhance your team's effectiveness and productivity.

Firstly, remember the mantra: 'Focus on less to achieve more.' This principle is particularly important when deciding on your team's MIGs. By narrowing your focus to a select few objectives, you can channel your team's energy and resources more effectively, leading to better outcomes. Ideally, each team should have no more than 2-3 MIGs. This allows for concentrated effort on each goal, ensuring that none are neglected or overlooked.

Secondly, ensure that your MIGs are measurable, ideally monthly. This aligns with the concept of SMART goals. By setting measurable goals, you can track your team's progress, identify areas for improvement, and celebrate successes along the way. This not only keeps your team motivated but also provides a clear direction and a sense of purpose.

Embedding these principles into your leadership strategy can dramatically boost your team's productivity and performance. It's crucial to ensure that the goals you set are effective and focused. Overloading your team with too many objectives or setting immeasurable goals can lead to confusion and frustration, hindering progress.

Throughout the rest of this book, you'll find a wealth of resources to guide you in this process. This includes examples of goals for various types of teams, as well as practical tips and strategies for those who may struggle to identify measurable objectives. This guidance is designed to give you the tools you need to lead your team effectively and navigate the path to success.

INTERPLAY BETWEEN INITIATIVES
AND KEY ACTIVITIES

Once you've established your team's goals, the next step is to identify the Key Activities. This is where Strategic Initiatives come into play. Some teams play a crucial role in enabling these initiatives, and discussing these is a natural part of any input conversation.

As a leader, you're often responsible for launching and securing buy-in for these initiatives within your team. Sometimes, these initiatives align seamlessly with your team's own agenda and are perceived as a natural part of their work. In these cases, the conversation can focus more on information sharing and breaking down the initiatives into achievable milestones.

However, there may be times when these initiatives represent significant change. In these instances, you, as a leader, need to pay special attention to how you present their necessity and what they might require from your team. If you find yourself in this situation, remember the principles we've already discussed.

Focus on explaining why these changes matter, and lead by example. Your actions can inspire your team to embrace these changes and follow suit. Your team looks to you for guidance and direction, so show them the way.

NAVIGATING NEW HORIZONS

Alex, usually a whirlwind of action and big ideas, found himself deeply engaged in the structured process, a shift from his typical approach. Acknowledging his past impulsiveness and its resulting missteps, Alex privately committed to embracing this new way of working, aiming to step up during the company's time of need.

Despite the initial unfamiliarity, Alex felt a sense of achievement as he saw the positive outcomes rapidly unfolding. His team's workshop had been particularly successful, and Alex was energized by the enthusiasm he saw around him. Embracing his role as a figurehead for this change, Alex actively participated in further workshops, feeling energized by the lively discussions and innovative ideas. His involvement was more than just symbolic; it was a commitment to his own growth and a testament to his ability to adapt and lead effectively.

Today, he and Jessica were facilitating a workshop for the Scandinavian field sales team. Spread across three geographical areas, the team consisted of about 20 sales representatives, each region led by a local team leader. Alex, Jessica and the team leaders had held a preparatory call three days prior, outlining the process and brainstorming some initial ideas to gently guide the group. They agreed on the importance of the workshop as a platform for the team to feel a sense of ownership over the ideas generated.

Being smaller sales teams, they weren't plagued by the typical silo mentality that was the norm in other parts of his organization. However, their Key Account Management practices lacked the maturity seen elsewhere. In fact, these local teams had a narrow focus, primarily selling only one or two products from their extensive range. This left potential for revenue increase through cross-selling to their larger clients largely untapped, a challenge that Alex had already addressed in other teams.

Furthermore, a considerable number of the sales staff had come onboard three years ago through an acquisition. Alex had always sensed a degree of isolation between them and the rest of his group. This workshop presented a prime opportunity to integrate everyone into the company's culture and align their processes with his vision for the sales team.

Jessica would run the meeting, as she had done in other regions and would continue to do in the future. Alex's role was to reiterate the playing field and the rules of the game, as well as to provide insights into the management team's discussions. He believed that this transparency would foster trust and break down barriers, aligning perfectly with his leadership style.

In previous teams, the conversation around the MIGs and the Initiatives had been relatively straightforward. It typically involved translating the global sales budget into regional budgets, eliminating secondary goals, and positioning the initiatives as enablers rather than corporate buzzwords. The reception to this new approach had pleasantly surprised Alex. Many echoed the sentiment of the Management Team, appreciating the clarity that cut through the usual corporate jargon. The teams appreciated being involved in the process and responded by actively engaging in the discussions.

The most intriguing and occasionally challenging discussions revolved around Key Activities. It was evident that there were some seasoned veterans in Alex's team who needed guidance to adapt to new ways. Alex anticipated a similar scenario today. Jessica and the team leaders had warned him that this group valued their autonomy and generally resisted anything that smelled of surveillance or a demand for individual transparency. But having navigated this exercise a few times now, Alex felt confident. He admired how Jessica had skillfully handled the discussions so far, and he was eager to see how today's workshop would unfold.

The team logged on and Jessica began. "Welcome all, I'm glad to see that we are at full capacity today. It will be a high-paced workshop, and I hope all of you had a chance to read through the email I sent to you a week ago outlining some of the central concepts and the ambition of today's session." Some nods of agreement followed, but Alex noticed there were some confused faces in the group as well. "Great," he thought, "almost half of the room seems to have ignored the communication from last week. Well, we'll just have to take it a bit slower and expect some resistance from that group."

"Alright, let's kick this off," Jessica began, her eyes sparkling with enthusiasm. "For those who haven't had the pleasure, meet Alex. You already know who he is, but don't let his senior title give you stage fright today."

Choosing to set his irritation aside, Alex decided to match Jessica's enthusiasm, aiming to inspire the best from the group, regardless of whether some of them would rather be somewhere else. "Thanks, Jessica," he replied with a genuine smile. "I'm here today not just as a leader but as a collaborator. We're in this together."

Alex paused for a moment, choosing his words carefully to connect with his audience. "Here's the deal," he continued, his tone shifting to a more serious note. "What matters most is unity," he emphasized. "We've been scattered in the past, both myself and the company as a whole. We in the management team recognize our duty to drive positive change. A key part of this is honing in on what really matters, cutting through the clutter. We aim for everyone to engage in meaningful tasks that contribute to our larger mission."

Seeing nods from the team, he continued, "This might sound like management jargon, but today we're turning it into reality. We're focusing on impactful tasks and letting go of the less critical ones. This approach has already been effective in other teams, fostering a sense of unity and purpose."

He continued, "We've heard your concerns about having too many goals and not knowing what's most important. We agree. So, we're going to focus on a few key things to make it easier for everyone." Alex then gave a straightforward rundown of the company's main goals and the steps to achieve them, before passing the baton back to Jessica.

Aware that some participants might not yet fully grasp the various concepts, having overlooked the pre-meeting briefings, Jessica dedicated the first 15 minutes to explaining the working methodology. She ensured that everyone understood the concepts of MIGs, Strategic Initiatives and Key Activities. The simplicity of the concept started to draw even the most hesitant members of the group into the discussion.

Next, she guided the group toward determining their team's MIGs. She followed the principles she had been taught by initiating a brainstorming session, separating outcomes from inputs, refining the ideas and, finally, voting. As anticipated, the group quickly agreed on focusing on generating new revenue, particularly from product lines they usually overlooked, and expanding their top 50 customers measured as revenue.

ACTIVITY-BASED STEERING

In the world of business, steering on Key Activities is not just a good idea, it's a great one. This practice, emanating from a concept often referred to as 'activity-based steering,' is a powerful tool that can transform the way teams work and how organizations function.

The true potential for transformation, however, lies within the broad segment of your workforce – the often-overlooked middle tier. These individuals, brimming with potential, have the capacity to elevate their performance to match that of your top achievers. They are the silent engine of your organization, capable of generating momentum that can shift the entire performance curve upward.

Envision a company where this central majority is empowered by a clear understanding of the Key Activities essential for success. Activity-based steering becomes the catalyst, aligning their daily efforts with strategic imperatives. Each member of the team gains a lucid appreciation of their role in the grand scheme, threading their day-to-day actions with the strategic goals of the company.

The ripple effect of this alignment is a collective elevation in performance and is the most impactful element behind the Execution Revolution. As the central workforce begins to mirror the excellence of the top performers, the organization's average performance level rises. Here, in this revolution, the 'middle' isn't just middle – it's the new centre of excellence, propelling us toward collective triumphs and a heightened standard of achievement.

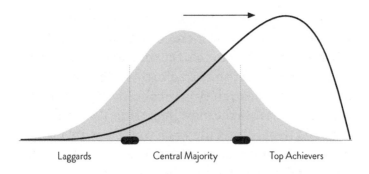

Laggards   Central Majority   Top Achievers

This approach is about creating a culture where every contribution is purposeful and measured. It's about fostering an environment where the progress of each Key Activity is a step towards the summit of strategic achievement.

It seems like a pretty efficient way to reach your destination, right? But here's the catch: many companies are still in the early stages of adopting this practice. Typically, only a few departments, like sales or engineering, have recognized its power and integrated it into their workflow.

Sales teams, for instance, often steer staff by the number of booked customer meetings, a precursor to new sales. Engineering and development teams, well-versed in the agile framework, are adept at breaking down goals and outputs and prioritizing them based on impact.

For many other teams, this structured approach to steering activities and identifying what actually makes a difference is a novel concept. While many teams appreciate the clarity it brings to their work, others may resist the newfound transparency. This clarity can quickly highlight who is doing the work and who is merely creating smoke screens.

As a manager, this is a powerful tool. It allows you to apply pressure where it's needed the most and clarify what actions matter to you, the company and the team. The element of peer pressure also comes into play. You're all in the same boat, and you've collectively decided that these activities are the most impactful. Therefore, failing to do them, especially when your peers are managing to incorporate them into their daily work, quickly becomes frowned upon by the whole group. This can nudge some of the laggards over the edge to finally fall in line.

However, as with any behavioural change, expect some resistance. It's natural for there to be pushback. The form it will take is hard to predict, but in a later chapter, I will explore the types of resistance you may face and how to handle them.

A MODERN PERFORMANCE MANAGEMENT SYSTEM

Consider, for a moment, the potential enhancements to traditional performance management systems this might bring. In many companies, the norm is to delegate responsibility to managers and steer the organization based on outcomes. This approach can work well in stable market conditions, where managers are free to manage their P&L as they see fit, as long as they deliver the expected results.

In recent years, we've seen an unprecedented level of disruption across various sectors, coupled with a downturn in market performance. In such challenging times, steering based on Key Activities should become a fundamental part of performance management systems in order to adapt successfully to changing and volatile conditions. This practice can significantly boost efficiency and productivity, providing a more proactive and effective way to align the company's efforts with its priorities. It's like driving your car while looking out of the front window, rather than relying solely on the rear-view mirror.

But let me be clear: ***this is not an argument for micro-managing*** every activity within the company. That would quickly become unmanageable and counterproductive. Instead, I'm suggesting that teams, aligned with company goals and initiatives, identify a few high-impact actions – the Key Activities – and use these as a basis for steering and monitoring progress.

This approach results in a highly effective, future-proof and resilient performance management system that can serve as a powerful tool for navigating the complexities of today's business landscape.

FACILITATING KEY ACTIVITIES

Back in the conference room, Alex, Jessica and the Scandinavian team shifted their conversation toward the actions necessary to achieve their goals. The brainstorming session had produced a list of 10 potential focus areas, which had been refined from the previous outcome-oriented discussion. The list included more client meetings, training on new product lines, implementing their new CRM-system, updating testimonials, and launching a customer loyalty club. While the list was a good start, Jessica had a gut instinct that told her it wasn't great. Yet.

Jessica felt that the list was too comfortable and familiar. It was filled with tasks the team would naturally do regardless. Jessica wanted the Key Activities to apply pressure on important and proactive tasks, and push the team out of their comfort zone.

The most critical improvement for the team, from Jessica's perspective, was to introduce more business lines per customer. This was directly linked to a prioritized Strategic Initiative and would be an excellent focus area to boost their sales with great long-term potential. To do this, they needed to gain access to more senior business stakeholders on the client's side, not just the usual lower-level contacts they were comfortable with. Only by reaching higher up could they engage stakeholders with the right decision-making authority for their diverse offerings.

Jessica was aware of the team's resistance to this idea. They weren't comfortable with these kinds of senior meetings, nor did they particularly enjoy initiating new meetings with unknown contacts. This was probably a common issue within sales departments, but it was a hurdle they needed to overcome. Jessica knew she needed to be tactful when positioning this suggestion, understanding the team's dynamics and their natural inclinations. She needed to guide them toward this new approach, not force them into it. It was a delicate balance, but one she was confident she could achieve.

Jessica decided to anchor her discussion around the distinction between General Activities and Key Activities in the context of their current conversation. They needed to identify their levers for a radical performance boost, not just the incremental enhancements of their daily operations.

"If we could take a step back," she began, her tone inviting and open, "what do we think could truly increase the chances of all our top 50 clients buying our full suite of offerings? What would be the game-changer that we'd point to two years from now?" She turned her gaze to the Norwegian Team Leader and asked, "Hugo, in your opinion, why do we typically close deals only for one business area?"

Hugo paused, a hint of discomfort crossing his face as he found himself in the spotlight. "Well, Jessica, I don't really know. Our stakeholders usually only need one product line for their department. It's typically different stakeholders for all our different products. For a large customer, we might need to talk to 10 or 15 people if we want to sell our full suite. It's time-consuming and often becomes very complex. I guess we prefer signing a straightforward deal without all the hassle. I mean, quicker money, right?"

Jessica nodded, appreciating Hugo's honesty, even though his perspective didn't align with hers. She knew she had a crucial point to make about reaching higher and not spreading thinly across 15 stakeholders. Everyone had a boss, and the boss usually had a broader view. But before she could articulate her thoughts, Erika, Hugo's Swedish counterpart, chimed in. "I agree with the first part of your thinking, Hugo. Our usual stakeholder only wants to buy something pretty narrow. But if we take Jessica's question seriously, what if we specifically targeted our usual stakeholder's manager? They are close enough to understand the need, but they also usually oversee other people using different product offerings. Maybe targeting them could help us land larger deals more naturally. The only problem is, they don't usually take our meetings. It's not like we haven't tried before."

Jessica listened, her eyes lighting up with the spark of a challenge. This was the hurdle they needed to overcome.

"Excellent," Jessica responded, her voice ringing with enthusiasm, "let's hypothetically assume that we CAN gain access and establish relevance at a higher level. Would this be a game-changer for your teams? What are your thoughts?" She noticed the nods of agreement, some hesitant, others more eager, but sensing the momentum, Jessica decided to drive the point home. "Why would that be, Erika?"

"Well," Erika began, her tone thoughtful, "besides what I mentioned earlier, there are possible benefits. The most significant one, of course, being the potential for larger deals. But I also suspect that these higher-level stakeholders don't interact with our competitors as much. So, we would have less competition targeting them. Also, if we position our offers in a way that demonstrates how we can save them money compared to their current solutions, I believe we wouldn't face as much pressure on our margins as we currently do."

Jessica nodded, appreciating Erika's insights. She decided to get more specific. "So, who are these people? At what level are you currently doing business, and who would be the right manager to sell toward instead?" After some discussion, they agreed that, IF they could do it – and it was a big if and a stretch – the C-suite level of their customers would be the ones to target. Jessica picked up her pen and wrote down their first Key Activity.

KEY ACTIVITY
Book C-suite stakeholders

DEFINITION OF DONE
Proactive sales meetings with C-suite stakeholders at any of our top 50 clients. Agenda is to introduce more business lines versus what they are currently using.

THE BOLD LEADER'S GUIDANCE

Consider what Jessica just put her team through. It's a path many leaders have trodden before – the quest to ignite change within their team. Jessica's team, a traditional sales force, found themselves in a familiar dance with the same stakeholders as their competitors, often settling for smaller, price-pressured deals.

This scenario, as common as it is, was playing out across the entire organization. Siloed product lines, each in their own world, rarely expanding their reach to potential big clients. It's a common issue for many product-oriented businesses, and often the starting point for initiatives focused on customer centricity and expansion.

Indeed, as with many aspects of life, the concept itself is simpler than its execution. Changing this dynamic necessitates a tailored approach, one that is sensitive to the unique dynamics of each team. The issue, deeply rooted in the allure of shortcuts and the comfort of 'business as usual,' must be tackled at its core – the behavioural level. The rush to close a deal, even if it's smaller than ideal, and the hesitation to extend their reach to higher-level stakeholders, are behaviours that need to be recalibrated.

Whether or not this specific example resonates with your unique circumstances, the underlying insight is universal. Every team has potential for improvement, which can be unlocked by fine-tuning behaviours. The challenge lies in identifying the right levers to pull and securing your team's commitment to the change.

As a leader, it's crucial to remember that the solution isn't something you simply tell your team. Instead, it's a destination you guide them toward, challenging them to find the path themselves. This may seem like a rounda-bout way to reach your goal, but the real battle lies in the execution of the plan. If your team only half-heartedly buys into the plan from the outset, you'll face a sea of excuses when it comes to implementation.

> *"The pessimist complains about the wind.*
> *The optimist expects it to change.*
> *The leader adjusts the sails."*
>
> **– JOHN MAXWELL.**

John C. Maxwell, an American author, speaker and pastor, is renowned for his contributions to leadership literature. With many bestsellers to his name, such as *The 21 Irrefutable Laws of Leadership* and *The 21 Indispensable Qualities of a Leader,* Maxwell has left an enduring impact in the domain of leadership and personal development.

But here's the interesting part. When the team is involved in setting the MIGs and Key Activities, they become invested in them. It becomes diffi-cult for any team member to deviate from the plan, because they were part of its creation. This dynamic is powerful, especially when you're trying to bring about change.

The concrete nature of Key Activities also has a significant impact. In many strategic workshops, the room buzzes with energy and ideas. But without a sense of scarcity and forced prioritization, there are often too many ideas and too little time to refine them into actionable tasks. This can lead to confusion and a lack of ownership. But when you're forced to pin down a few Key Activities, you have the time to define what 'done' looks like.

DEFINITION OF DONE

Clarity is a necessity. One of the most potent tools a leader can wield to cultivate this clarity is the 'Definition of Done.' Borrowed from the spheres of project management and software development, this concept serves as a clear, concise declaration of what completion looks like for a task or project. It's a finish line that's visible and comprehensible to everyone on the team.

The Definition of Done plays a pivotal role in several ways. First and foremost, it establishes a shared understanding of what success entails. When every team member knows precisely what they're striving for, it dispels ambiguity and ensures everyone is rowing in the same direction. This shared vision is a potent motivator and can significantly bolster team cohesion and productivity.

Secondly, a distinct Definition of Done helps manage expectations. It sets a benchmark for quality and ensures everyone understands what's expected of them. This can preempt misunderstandings and conflicts, ensuring everyone is held to the same standard. It also helps eliminate the need for rework, a common pitfall for less aligned teams and leaders.

Thirdly, it provides a clear reference point for tracking progress. By defining what completion looks like for a task, it becomes much simpler to gauge how far you've come and how far you still have to go. It also allows for a confident declaration of completion, freeing up resources to focus on other tasks. This can be a powerful tool for maintaining momentum and keeping the team focused and motivated.

However, a Definition of Done is more than just a tool for managing tasks and projects. It's a reflection of the leader's approach and mindset. Effective leaders understand that their role isn't just about getting things done quickly, but about getting them done right. They recognize that while efficiency is important, it should never compromise effectiveness. When leaders prioritize effectiveness over efficiency, it results in clearer communication, fewer misunderstandings and, ultimately, superior results.

A well-defined Definition of Done ensures focus on effectiveness. It encourages the team to not just complete tasks, but to complete them to a high standard. It advocates for quality over quantity and depth over breadth.

By defining what completion looks like for a task, leaders can ensure that their teams are not just working hard but working smart. They can make sure that their teams are not just doing things right, but doing the right things.

QUALITY AND QUANTITY

When we start working with a Key Activity, it applies a consistent pressure at the exact point where behavioural resistance is strongest. Let's consider the analogy of physical training. Most of us acknowledge the benefits of exercise – it's good for our health, minds and our overall wellbeing. Yet, many of us struggle to make it to the gym, despite enjoying the experience once we're there. In this context, the Key Activity could be as simple as "Go to the Gym." It doesn't need to be more complex than that. A straightforward strategy, executed well, will always outperform a sophisticated one that's poorly implemented. We will delve into the execution aspect, but for now, focus on identifying the weak spots in your core processes and the behaviours that need to be addressed.

Often, it's about doing more of something beneficial. It's a behaviour everyone agrees is valuable, but it's challenging to maintain and, therefore, isn't executed frequently enough to make a significant impact. This could be the number of training sessions you manage to fit into your week, or in a sales context, it could be about securing more meetings with relevant stakeholders than before. The focus is on increasing the volume of opportunities, or as the legendary Wayne Gretzky put it:

"You miss 100% of the shots you don't take."
– WAYNE GRETZKY

Wayne Gretzky is a legendary figure in the world of ice hockey. With numerous records and accolades to his name, he is widely regarded as one of the greatest hockey players in history.

However, quantity without quality is meaningless. If you spend your entire gym session scrolling through your phone, you won't make much progress. Similarly, in sales, meeting the right stakeholders is often more important than the volume of stakeholders. Therefore, the quality aspect is equally, if not more, important in deriving value from a Key Activity.

Focus on output rather than input. For example, "Book C-suite Stakeholders" is a more effective Key Activity than "Cold-Calling C-suite Stakeholders." This approach emphasizes the specific value of the Key Activity, and it recognizes that there are multiple paths to the same destination. As a leader, the specific path chosen often doesn't matter. However, if you focus on the input variable, you risk your team claiming they've put in more effort than they have. It's nearly impossible to accurately measure input, and it can quickly become an excuse for avoiding the behaviour by exaggerating the amount of input generated. As a leader, you can circumvent this temptation by emphasizing the process output, effectively eliminating the problem.

THE ANATOMY OF A KEY ACTIVITY

A Key Activity is a potent blend of qualitative and quantitative elements. It's a strategic action, meticulously designed with four integral components:
1. Title
2. Purpose (Description)
3. Definition of Done
4. Recurring Numeric Goal

The **Title** is the identity of the activity. It's succinct, memorable and precise enough to set the Key Activity apart from routine tasks. For instance, "Booking meetings" is less meaningful than "Book C-suite Stakeholders."

The **Purpose** is the rationale behind choosing this activity over others. It's the reminder of the strategic thinking that went into its selection during the workshop. It outlines the business logic the Key Activity is intended to drive. For example:

> "To elevate our average deal size and secure multi-line business from our larger customers, we need to engage with more senior stakeholders. These individuals wield broader control and larger budgets. This Key Activity is focused on securing meetings with our top 50 clients, as they hold the greatest potential for expansion."

The **Definition of Done** is the quality assurance for the Key Activity. It outlines the criteria that must be met for the activity to be considered complete. Only efforts that meet this definition count toward the team goal, ensuring all efforts align with the team's MIGs. For instance:

> *"Proactive sales meetings with C-suite stakeholders at any of our top 50 clients, with the agenda to introduce more business lines than they are currently utilizing."*

This approach to Key Activities ensures that every action is strategic, purposeful and contributes directly to achieving the team's MIGs.

Lastly, the **Recurring Numeric Goal** sets the pace. It determines the volume of the Key Activity needed to significantly impact the MIG.

The debate between team goals and individual goals is a well-researched topic, with notable contributions from Edwin Locke and Gary Latham. Both team and individual goal setting have their merits and are best used together. Team goals can foster cooperation, encourage information sharing, and create a sense of collective responsibility. Individual goals, on the other hand, can enhance personal accountability and motivation.

The beauty of the Key Activities system, as you'll discover in the upcoming chapters, is its ability to harmonize both team and individual goals. The ideal process involves setting a weekly team goal, often reverse-engineered based on what's needed to reach the MIG. This team activity goal is then broken down weekly into individual contributions, satisfying the personal aspect. This approach lends flexibility to the performance management system, allowing for adjustments based on team members' availability and fostering a sense of collective effort.

The goal is articulated as a numeric target with a clear unit of measurement. For instance, in our sales example, the goal might be:

"Four booked meetings per week per team."

Over half a year, an eight-member team would book over 100 meetings with senior stakeholders at their most important clients – meetings that wouldn't otherwise have happened. From an individual perspective, it averages out to just one new stakeholder every other week – a manageable workload for someone just starting to book different stakeholders.

CHAPTER 5
PRIORITIZING TOMORROW, TODAY

Alex felt a newfound sense of unity within his organization. They were at the beginning of their journey, yet they had already covered significant ground. The sense of progress was clear, the momentum undeniable.

Alex had been a part of more than half the workshops, a decision that had required a significant investment of his time. He knew his peers in the company's management team had made different choices, some following his lead, others charting their own course. He looked forward to the upcoming discussions, the exchange of experiences and the shared learnings. But today, his focus was on his own team.

The management team had set out a clear implementation plan. They had decided to drive the process from the top, setting the priorities and ensuring buy-in at each level of the hierarchy. At the same time, they had encouraged bottom-up engagement, giving each team the autonomy to decide how they could best contribute to the overarching MIGs and what Key Activities they needed to focus on.

The process was a dance between top-down direction and bottom-up initiative.

Now, with all the workshops completed, the day's agenda was to bring it all together by aligning the teams, learning from each other, identifying potential risks and roadblocks, and finally, deciding on their own team's Key Activities.

They had consciously held back on defining their own Key Activities until this part of the process, focusing their initial efforts on securing buy-in for the methodology. They knew that many of the challenges identified by the teams would ultimately fall to them to address. Today was the day they would step into that role, providing the guidance and solutions their teams were looking for. Since Alex had spoken to his managers before today's session, he could feel the anticipation and shared sense of purpose. Today, they would move forward, together.

SHARED EXPERIENCES

"Hello, everyone! I'm thrilled to see you all here. We've all put in a lot of effort, and I want to take a moment to thank you all for your contributions. I really mean it," Alex began.

"It's not often that we, as leaders, find ourselves in a situation like this. In a very short period of time, we've been introduced to a new methodology and tasked with implementing it within our respective teams. And at the heart of it all, we've had to grapple with tough choices, resistance, tactical decisions, and a whole lot of rallying and inspiring. What fills me with pride is the fact that we've seen more champions than skeptics."

Alex's words resonated in the room, a warm acknowledgment of the team's hard work and dedication. The group responded with nods and smiles, their faces reflecting pride and gratitude. "I want to start off by hearing your reflections from the past months. I asked you all to come prepared for this discussion. I'm not looking for yes-men or yes-women. I want this session to underscore that we're in this together, that we can learn from the successes of our colleagues and acknowledge our own shortcomings. We can only grow if we recognize that we're all on a journey of discovery. I make a lot of mistakes, so I don't expect perfection from you. What I do expect is that we give it our all and that we're systematic in learning from our actions, so we don't repeat the same mistakes. Are we all on board with that?"

The room responded with more nods. Alex was often driven by impulse, sometimes to a fault, but when it mattered the most, he was thoughtful and deliberate. His charisma and authenticity had fostered an environment where his team felt comfortable letting their guard down.

REVISITING AND REVISING

"Let's start with marketing," Alex continued, turning to Josh. Josh had a calm and steady presence that commanded respect. As the Chief Marketing Officer, he had a knack for spotting trends and inspiring his team.

He leaned back in his chair, and said, "Alex, as you know, we've had a lot of workshops. With my teams at the headquarters and the regional teams, we've had a lot to coordinate. Most of our teams took to the new methodology like fish to water. But our creative teams ... well, let's just say they had some unique interpretations of 'measurable goals.' One team argued that you can't measure great content. I told them that's like a chef saying you can't tell if food tastes good."

A ripple of laughter went through the room. Josh smiled and continued. "In hindsight, I think I could have directed my efforts more effectively. Some of our managers needed more support than others, and I regret not being there for them as much as I should have been. I also realize now that I could have predicted some of these challenges based on our initial reactions to the new methodology."

THE FACE OF SUBTLE RESISTANCE

Josh's voice trailed off, and he sighed. His gaze drifted, as if he was looking at something only he could see. "And then there's Luc," he began, a note of uncertainty creeping into his voice. "Luc, who's in charge of our Brand Management. Some of you might know him already."

He looked back at the group, and said, "Luc just doesn't seem to get it. He keeps asking questions, but it's ... it's different. It feels like he's not trying to understand, but rather ... delay. Like he's throwing pebbles in our path, not to trip us up, but to slow us down. And I can't quite figure out why."

He asked, "Is it resistance to change? A lack of understanding? Or is it something else entirely? I'm grappling with this, trying to work out what he's trying to achieve. And I'm not sure how to handle it."

Feeling frustrated and concerned, he looked around at his colleagues and admitted, "I could really use some advice on this one."

The room was quiet after Josh's plea for advice. The tension hung heavy in the air until, from the corner of the room, a voice cut through the silence.

"Have you tried the old 'fit in or fuck off' attitude with him?" asked Martin, the Director of Sales Operations. His tone was blunt, his words a stark contrast to the reflective atmosphere Alex had fostered. Martin was known for his no-nonsense approach, his crass humour often at odds with the warmer nature of the other leaders.

Elinor, ever the diplomat, immediately reacted. Her eyes widened at Martin's words, a gasp escaping her lips. She quickly composed herself, smoothing out her surprise with a more measured response.

"Martin!" Elinor exclaimed. "That's a bit like using a sledgehammer to crack a nut, don't you think?" She turned to Josh, her expression softening. "What Martin is trying to say, in his unique way, is that a direct approach can sometimes be effective.

If Luc is not on board with the new methodology, it might be worth having a frank conversation with him about his concerns and his role in the team. But has it been long enough to make that call? It's only been a month, after all."

Josh nodded. "You're right, Elinor. I've only recently realized that there might be more to Luc's behaviour than just a slow pick-up of the concept. I have a meeting planned with him soon, and I need some advice on how to handle it."

Alex, who had been listening quietly, finally spoke up. His voice was calm and reassuring, a steady presence in the room. "Josh, being straightforward is usually the best course of action. You could say something like, 'Luc, I've noticed that you're not fully bought in, and I want to know why.' It's possible that Luc is just afraid of being caught off guard in front of his team. After all, this is a change journey, and he doesn't have all the answers yet."

Alex leaned back in his chair, a twinkle in his eye. "And let's be honest, who among us hasn't been afraid of being caught with our pants down at some point? My point is that's it's okay not to have all the answers, but avoiding accountability through sidelining yourself isn't. Let's focus on letting Luc know that driving this type of change is expected of him as a leader but give him the security of us backing him up as long as we see him trying."

EXPECT RESISTANCE, FOSTER OWNERSHIP

Resistance to change is common with both managers and employees. The challenge of adapting to new circumstances and shifting priorities can be daunting. While it's natural to occasionally resist change, this resistance often stems from an individual's difficulty in adjusting to new scenarios. This inability to adapt can significantly hinder strategy execution.

Research has shown that a staggering 90% of Strategic Initiatives fail[1] to achieve their projected financial gains within the expected timeframe. This inefficiency translates to a significant economic loss. To put it in perspective, organizations worldwide waste approximately $1 million every 20 seconds due to ineffective strategy implementation.[2] Addressing this inefficiency is paramount for business leaders. Fostering your leaders' ability to engage their teams effectively and communicate your strategy clearly to ensure rapid, enthusiastic buy-in is a win or lose question.

Reflect for a moment on the vast, untapped potential, the groundbreaking innovations that never see the light of day, the invaluable public resources squandered without yielding tangible benefits, and the pressing global issues like climate change that continue to intensify, demanding our immediate attention and action. Each missed step not only represents a setback for businesses but also has broader implications for our communities, our environment and future generations. These issues could be tackled far more effectively if the principles championed by the Execution Revolution were more widely adopted.

THE RECIPE

The room was buzzing as each team took turns presenting their MIGs and Key Activities. It was testament to the newly-adopted 'less is more' attitude. Teams had distilled their ambitions into a focused set of 2-3 MIGs, each with a corresponding 1-2 Key Activities. It was a far cry from the sprawling, unfocused goals of the past.

As the presentations were given, it was clear that some teams were deeply entwined in company-wide initiatives, while others had a more niche focus. The diversity of roles and responsibilities within the teams was mirrored in their MIGs and Key Activities, creating a rich tapestry of the Sales and Marketing division's concerted efforts.

Jessica, surveying the slides, felt a sense of pride. "A year ago, we would have been drowning in a sea of vague, unattainable goals," she mused, her voice carrying the weight of experience. "Now, we've got a clear road map. No fluff, just focused, action-able targets."

Elinor, ever the pragmatist, nodded in agreement. "And it all fits together like a well-oiled machine," she added. "Each team's goals and actions are aligned with the broader Sales and Market-ing MIG. It's a far cry from the chaotic jigsaw puzzle we used to call our strategy."

However, the process wasn't without its hiccups. A few teams had missed the mark on their MIGs and Key Activities. The issue typically lay in overlooking important dependencies between teams, which had been highlighted during previous discussions. It served as a reminder that setting goals was only part of the process; ensuring alignment with the overall strategy and other teams was equally crucial.

Despite some bumps in the road, the feedback was taken on board. Both Josh and Martin acknowledged the need for adjust-ments in their teams and committed to revising their MIGs and Key Activities. The willingness to learn and improve was clear to everyone.

The meeting was not just about setting and aligning goals, but also for sharing knowledge and insights. The team leaders found new respect for each other's challenges and achievements, and the atmosphere was one of mutual support. They shared their highs and lows, offering advice and encouragement. By the end of the meeting, there was a clear understanding of the collective goals and actions, and a renewed sense of purpose and commitment.

RECURRING VERSUS NON-RECURRING KEY ACTIVITIES

There are two types of Key Activity that drive outcomes. The first, which we've been discussing, is the Recurring Key Activity. These are tasks that we perform on a regular basis, sometimes multiple times every week. They're the drumbeat of our improvements, the steady rhythm that keeps us moving forward. These activities are particularly effective in driving a necessary behaviour change within the team. They're the spotlight that illuminates the weak links in our core processes and helps us overcome resistance to change.

The essence of a Recurring Key Activity is beautifully captured in a quote that has echoed through the ages, surviving for over two millennia:

"We are what we repeatedly do.
Excellence then, is not a single act,
but a habit."

– ARISTOTLE

Aristotle, the ancient Greek philosopher, left a lasting legacy in philosophy and ethics. His profound teachings significantly shaped our understanding of excellence and emphasized personal responsibility in achieving it.

These words, spoken by Aristotle around 350 BC, resonate deeply with the concept of Recurring Key Activities. They remind us that our habits shape our identity, and that by focusing on the right tasks, we can steer our team toward excellence.

The second type of Key Activity is more suited to teams that operate without a central repeating process. This could include management teams, business development teams, project-based work teams or engineering teams. For these teams, each activity is a unique endeavour, requiring more planning and coordination, but offering more flexibility in return.

Strategic tasks share some characteristics with their recurring counterparts. They have a Title that explains what needs to be achieved and a Definition of Done. But that's where the similarities end. Instead of a weekly goal, each one-off Key Activity has its own deadline. And instead of a shared goal, these Key Activities are individually owned.

For instance, let's consider our sales team from earlier. They identified a need to become relevant to new stakeholders. This might require a couple of Key Activities connected to this initiative. Each of these Key Activities would be unique, but all would contribute to the overall Strategic Initiative of expanding existing clients through more business lines per client.

DEVELOP STAKEHOLDER MAPPING STRATEGY

Definition of Done: The Key Account Director has, via all local KAMs, identified key senior stakeholders within each existing and potential client organization, and has outlined a clear strategy for building and maintaining relationships with them.

CONDUCT ADVANCED COMMUNICATION SKILLS WORKSHOP

Definition of Done: The Regional Sales Manager has organized and successfully executed a workshop focusing on advanced communication skills, specifically tailored to engage with senior stakeholders.

IMPLEMENT STRATEGIC SELLING TECHNIQUES

Definition of Done: The Sales Director has established a formal process for aligning the features and benefits of our solutions with the long-term strategic goals of senior stakeholders, highlighting the value of our offer in terms of the client's scorecard.

COMPLETE EXECUTIVE PRESENCE TRAINING

Definition of Done: The Regional Sales Director has contracted a qualified external agency or in-house expert to conduct an 'Executive Presence' training course for the sales team.

PLANNING HORIZONS AND STRATEGIC TASK MANAGEMENT

In strategic task management, foresight and coordination are paramount. Yet, it is often the flexibility within any plan that can make it excel in the wild. However, this flexibility can sometimes lead to an ad-hoc mentality, reducing strategic tasks to a mere operational checklist. While this may enhance transparency and allow for effective delegation, it often fails to significantly advance strategic objectives. Therefore, it's crucial to consider how different planning horizons will influence the efficacy of your plan.

Project management methodologies range from the highly structured waterfall approach to the spontaneous ad-hoc style. Waterfall planning, characterized by meticulous detail and long-term forecasts, has seen a decline in popularity. Its rigidity often clashes with the need for adaptability, leading to a burdensome cycle of replanning whenever reality deviates from the plan.

*"Everyone has a plan until they
get punched in the face."*

– MIKE TYSON

Mike Tyson is a former professional boxer who is widely regarded as one of the greatest heavyweight fighters in the history of boxing. Outside of boxing, Tyson has been involved in various business ventures, acting and entertainment. He remains a prominent figure in the world of sports and pop culture.

Conversely, ad-hoc planning, while nimble, can result in a frenzied environment where immediate tasks eclipse strategic goals.

Top-performing teams find a sweet spot between thoughtful planning and operational agility. They conscientiously deconstruct ambitious goals into manageable segments, operating within monthly or quarterly cycles. This structured yet adaptable framework ensures a steady progression toward each objective, mitigating the risk of being overwhelmed, and facilitating regular strategic assessments.

This planning methodology is designed to encourage teams to break down colossal tasks into digestible chunks. Think back to your school days and the looming threat of exams. There were always two camps: the night-before crammers and the steady studiers. Relying on a structured planning method is the academic equivalent of spacing out your study sessions over a month. It's the realization that burning the midnight oil right before a major project is a poor strategy. By segmenting the monumental task, the process becomes not only more bearable but also produces a far better outcome.

In the corporate world, this means the difference between successfully completed initiatives and projects perpetually stuck in 'almost done.' While rigid, long-term plans may quickly become outdated, the absence of planning can lead to a frantic rush to meet deadlines, often resulting in subpar outcomes.

> *"Proper Prior Planning Prevents Piss Poor Performance."*
> – HER MAJESTY'S ARMED FORCES

A Strategic Planning Cycle is a designated period, ranging from a month to a quarter, during which a team commits to accomplishing specific Key Activities. These activities form a strategic checklist, focusing on the most impactful improvements toward the MIG.

The key to success lies in the planners' ability to periodically step back from day-to-day operations and contemplate the strategic agenda. By aligning tasks with the MIGs and Strategic Initiatives, teams can foster innovation and ambition that is seldom achieved through week-by-week planning.

The strategic focus extends beyond short-term achievements or incremental improvements. It's about making substantial progress toward goals that resonate with the team's overarching strategy, and prioritizing activities with the greatest strategic impact, rather than merely ticking off tasks.

These non-recurring Key Activities, whether complementing Recurring Key Activities or standing alone, are chosen for their strategic value. Teams may concentrate on a few central behaviours through Recurring Key Activities while pursuing several unique Key Activities.

This combination encourages a rhythm of behavioural improvements and strategic execution.

By adopting Strategic Planning Cycles, teams gain clarity and priority in their business plan progression. Tasks are organized logically, and the entire team engages in their execution, optimizing collective effort and efficiency.

This methodology not only ensures task completion but also cultivates a culture of shared responsibility and unity – essential elements for triumphant strategic execution.

This strategic method results in fewer, yet more significant, activities per person each cycle, contrasting with the traditional to-do list that often overloads individuals with minutiae. In this proposed concept, team members may have only a handful of Key Activities per month, underscoring their importance. These strategic tasks, typically only accounting for a portion of the week, ensure that strategic advancements are prioritized without micromanaging the individual contributors.

A WEEKLY COMMITMENT TO CLARITY AND COLLABORATION

Alex shifted his focus to the contributions his team needed to make on this journey. There was a clear sense of anticipation and responsibility as they delved into this discussion. They were not just observers in this process; they were active participants, and their actions would significantly influence the course of the company's future.

The team engaged in thoughtful dialogue about their role as the organization's management team. They pondered on what their contribution should promote, and how they could best support the company's initiatives. The conversation was marked by a shared understanding of the weight of their responsibilities and a commitment to fulfilling them.

Their work was divided into two categories. The first encompassed the tasks that the management team themselves needed to undertake to support the Strategic Initiatives that Sales and Marketing were working on. These included the expansion of existing clients through upselling and cross-selling, the implementation of the new CRM system, and the launch in the UK market.

The second category comprised activities that supported the organization, such as unblocking issues and clarifying decisions. It was evident that they lacked a process to capture, escalate and, ultimately, resolve these issues. The realization was met with a sense of urgency and determination to address this gap.

Alex and his team recognized that during such change-intensive periods, there were bound to be numerous interdependencies. They wanted to stay ahead of these, providing their organization with a swift resolution of risks. They saw this as one of their most crucial roles at this time. They also wanted to continue highlighting the learnings of their team and keep each other informed of decisions they made within the organization.

With these considerations in mind, they decided on a Recurring Key Activity, which they defined as follows:

MANAGEMENT WEEKLY ALIGNMENT

Purpose: To align and focus management on what is most important by providing a short report on overall status prior to each management team meeting. To reinforce learnings and share information.

DEFINITION OF DONE:

1. What risks / obstacles stand in the way of meeting your current deadlines?
2. Do you need assistance from other management members to mitigate these risks?
3. Any best / bad practices you want to share?
4. Any decisions you have made since the last meeting?

TWO FRESH IDEAS TO IMPROVE PLANNING

Alex began. "Alright folks, let's shift gears and dive into our development agenda and what other Key Activities we need to accomplish," he announced, his voice carrying a note of determination. The room fell silent, all eyes on him. "I want us to not just show up for these Strategic Initiatives, but knock them out of the park."

He continued, "Just to jog your memory, we've got three big fish to fry. First, we're going to squeeze every ounce of revenue we can from our largest clients. We're not just going to sell to them, we're going to become their go-to for everything we offer, leaving our competitors in the dust. I know this has been a hot topic in our team discussions. Second, we've got the new CRM system. It's a beast of a project, with data cleanup, process automation and training, and guess what? – it's mostly on us.

Lastly, we're going back to the UK. The decision's been made, and we need to make sure we hit the ground running."

Elinor, who had been quietly taking notes, looked up. She had seen this scenario play out before, where discussions became scattered and lost focus. "These discussions can sometimes be all over the place," she said, her voice steady and calm. "I suggest we go topic by topic, and don't try to juggle all the topics at the same time." They had all experienced meetings where the conversation had spiralled, leaving them with a sense of frustration and a lack of progress.

Alex appreciated Elinor's insight. He had been part of those meetings too, and he knew the cost of losing focus. "I agree," he said. "And I've got another idea to throw into the mix. Normally in planning, we end up feeling like we can't manage much change because of everything we already have going on. It's like our regular operations are a giant sponge, soaking up all our time. Does that sound familiar?"

With nods of agreement, he continued, "However, at this specific point in time, change is what matters, so we must find a way to squeeze these bigger movements into our already packed schedules. In the management team, we tried an exercise where we envisioned a moment in the future and had a discussion about what we need to have achieved by then to impact our MIG enough, rather than starting from today and moving forward. The result was a pretty drastic reshuffling of everyone's calendars because it became apparent there were bigger fish to fry."

His words hung in the air as the team absorbed the implications. It was a simple idea, but one that could fundamentally shift their approach to planning.

He continued, "We've all experienced the constraints of a calendar filled to the brim with tasks, leaving little room for strategic improvements. By starting from a point in the future and working our way back, we can prioritize what truly drives value, rather than just filling our calendars with tasks."

His words resonated with the team. Everyone had felt the pressure of a packed calendar, the constant juggling of tasks, and the frustration of not having enough time for strategic work. Alex's proposal offered a way out, a way to break free from the constraints of their calendars and focus on what truly mattered.

"I understand this means a change in your calendars," Alex said, his gaze steady. "I'm offering you carte blanche to critically evaluate how your time is currently spent. Stop doing things of lesser value, even if they are expected. As long as you are transparent about priorities, I'd prefer you to work on stuff that is actually important, versus the business as usual, low-value everyday tasks of a corporate manager."

PARKINSON'S LAW AND REVERSE ENGINEERED PLANNING

Planning and time management are the bedrock of any successful business strategy. However, the conventional approach of planning from today and moving forward often leads to calendars that are as crammed as a suitcase on the last day of a vacation, leaving no room for essential, strategic improvements.

Imagine you're preparing for an important journey, and your suitcase represents your planning calendar. Now, if you start by tossing in all the small, less critical items first – those impulse buys, the just-in-case gadgets, and all the minor things that clutter our lives – you might find there's no room left for the essentials. These are your strategic goals: the vital documents, the versatile outfits for important meetings, the gear that will ensure your trip is a success.

The art of packing, much like strategic planning, is knowing what to bring and what to leave behind. It's about placing the essentials in your suitcase first, ensuring they have a reserved spot. Then, and only then, if there's space, you can add other items – or decide they're not worth the extra weight. This is the essence of reverse-engineered planning: prioritizing the tasks that will have the most significant impact on reaching your destination successfully and being willing to leave behind what doesn't serve your journey's purpose.

*"Work expands so as to fill the time
available for its completion."*

– CYRIL NORTHCOTE PARKINSON

Cyril Northcote Parkinson, a British naval historian, popularized 'Parkinson's Law,' which humorously points out that work tends to expand to fill the time allotted for its completion. His keen observation on productivity and time management continues to influence how we perceive and manage tasks in various domains, emphasizing the importance of efficiency and deadlines.

Enter Parkinson's Law. In the context of a manager's calendar, this means that regardless of the actual workload, the calendar tends to get fully booked. This phenomenon often leads to managers being drawn into ad hoc meetings and agendas, and steered by circumstances rather than being in charge of their own priorities.

To navigate around this frustrating reality, an effective strategy is to reverse engineer the planning process. This involves envisioning a point in the future, typically three or six months ahead, and defining what needs to be true by then for the MIGs to be adequately impacted. From this future point, the process works backwards, asking what needs to be done each preceding month to make that future reality come true. It's like planning a journey, but instead of starting from where you are, you start from where you want to be.

This approach illuminates the strategic tasks that need to be prioritized, pushing lesser value tasks out of the calendar. The result is not an increase in workload, but a shift in focus. As managers stop doing the lesser value tasks, they move up in the value chain of their calendar, focusing more on strategic work at the expense of some operational tasks. This is a crucial shift, as many managers tend to be too operational and struggle to make time for strategy.

Consider a scenario where teams shift their perspective from being constrained by their calendars to being driven by their strategic objectives. The pace of strategic deployment doesn't just increase, it catapults forward with the force of a quantum leap.

This might seem like a small shift in thinking, but in practice, it's huge. At first, this transformation can feel uncomfortable. It requires saying no to lesser value tasks, and embracing a new way of thinking. But as this mindset matures, it becomes not just manageable, but enjoyable. As a manager, imagine the satisfaction of no longer being owned by your calendar, no longer being in reactive mode. Instead, you're in the driver's seat, spending time on tasks that really make a difference.

STRATEGIC PLANNING SESSIONS

This was the maiden voyage into the first Strategic Planning session as a team. The agenda was hefty: driving customer expansion, implementing the new CRM system and launching in the UK.

They decided to tackle one task at a time, starting with a strategy they'd playfully dubbed "reverse-engineered planning." Alex, taking the lead, suggested they dive into the UK Launch first. "Look," he began, "six months from now, we should be shaking hands with our first UK customer. Considering our usual 2-3-month sales cycle, especially if we start by targeting clients we're already familiar with in other regions, we've still got our work cut out. Top priority? Getting a sales team set up in the UK. Let's brainstorm the essentials. And just to keep everyone in the loop, we're already on the hunt for a local country manager, and the legal team is knee-deep in paperwork setting up the affiliate."

Jessica, with her finger on the pulse of European operations, jumped in. "First off, we need a local office, a base of operations," she pointed out, "and of course, a UK Sales Manager to steer the ship. Alex, have we crunched the numbers on staffing?"

Alex nodded, "We're thinking lean to begin with: one manager and a pair of field sales reps for the first half-year, just to test the water."

Jessica, ever pragmatic, responded, "Then we better get those positions filled ASAP. If we're aiming for them to hit the ground running in three months, time's ticking."

Alex grinned, "Exactly my thought. What else should we consider?"

Josh, always with an eye on branding, added, "We should draft a local marketing strategy. Maybe even host a launch event to make some noise. Martin, any hiccups with the CRM system we should be aware of?"

Martin, always the practical one, chimed in, "Look, there's a laundry list of things my team needs to sort out: system logins, setting up processes for the UK, integrating local data sources, and getting those planning templates and scorecards in order. But do we really need to get into the nitty-gritty here? Maybe we just need a broad activity label like 'UK Sales Support Ready' or something along those lines."

"You've got a point, Martin," Alex said. "We need to strike a balance. While we're crafting these Key Activities, we should consider the level of detail that's relevant for this group. There will be times when the specifics are handled by our teams, but here, we need to know if the job's done or if it's still hanging. We don't need a play-by-play. Are we all on the same page?"

Most heads nodded in agreement, but Jessica, playing devil's advocate, raised an eyebrow. "Isn't that a bit like doing the same job twice? One overarching activity here, which then splinters into five more detailed tasks for the teams below?"

Martin shot back, "It's up to each of us how we manage our tasks. The bottom line is that we have to get things done on schedule, right? If you want to divvy up tasks in your team, go for it. But in this room, we need to keep our eyes on the prize and the major deadlines. I don't see it as double work; it's about perspective. For instance, I need to ensure all systems are go for UK Launch. And I bet both you and Alex are keen to know they're ready when your UK team starts. So, I'm okay with reporting the big picture here. The specifics of who does what in my team? That's my circus and my monkeys. Honestly, Jess, I think we're talking apples and oranges here."

Alex, sensing the atmosphere getting more tense, decided to step in. "I get both perspectives. But let's remember, we're in a period of significant change, and during such times, transparency isn't just a buzzword – it's crucial. We've got to ensure we're all singing from the same song sheet. I want us, as a management team, to have a clear, unified picture. That way, we're always aligned on our Key Activities and there's no room for ambiguity. Jess, can you see the value in that approach?"

Jessica paused, processing Alex's words. Then, with a nod, she replied, "I get it, Alex. As long as we're clear on our approach and consistent in our actions, I'm on board. It does give me some wiggle room in my division, which is always appreciated. So, shall we get back to it? We were diving into the UK Launch, right?"

Over the next couple of hours, they meticulously mapped out their strategy for the UK Launch and other initiatives, ensuring every task was accounted for. By the end of the session, they had a clear road map for the next six months. While the immediate future was crystal clear, they acknowledged that the latter months would need further refining. To address this, they scheduled a follow-up session in three months.

CHAPTER 6
STRATEGY STAND-UPS AND BUILDING A CULTURE OF COMMITMENT

DREAMERS VERSUS DOERS

In many organizations, the challenge isn't just setting a goal. It's about achieving that critical goal while being constantly bombarded by daily tasks and urgencies. It's easy to get lost in this whirlwind and to let it sweep away our best-laid plans, but what if there was a way to harness this chaos?

Traditional accountability often feels punitive. It's that looming annual review or the dread of being reprimanded for a missed target. But what if accountability could be transformed into a positive, engaging experience? An experience where team members make personal commitments to each other, promising to take specific actions that drive the larger goal forward.

Imagine a weekly meeting, but not just any meeting. It's a 'Strategy Stand-Up,' where the only focus is on holding each other accountable for taking those crucial steps, for working on those Key Activities, that propel the MIG forward. There's no room for distractions here. The daily whirlwind, with its urgencies and fires to put out, is kept at bay. This meeting is a sanctuary, a space where the team only talks about and commits to actions that will move the needle.

And these aren't just any actions. They're influence-able, specific steps that an individual can take, which in turn predictably drive the MIG. It's a chain reaction, where each link is crucial, from the individual's weekly commitment to the Key Activity, all the way to the overarching MIG.

TODAY ———————————————— 1 YEAR

A dream written down with a clear date
becomes a goal.

TODAY - - - - - - - - - - - - - - - - - - - 1 YEAR

A goal broken down into steps
becomes a plan.

TODAY - - - - - - - - - - - - - - - - - - - 1 YEAR

A dream backed by action makes your
dreams come true.

In this world, accountability isn't a burden; it's a promise. It's a promise to ourselves and to the team. It's the bridge between dreaming and doing, between setting a goal and achieving it. The Strategy Stand-Up isn't about grand plans; its focus is on actionable steps.

It's the bridge between the dreamer who says, "I wish to," and the doer who says, "I will."

"The secret of getting ahead is getting started."

– MARK TWAIN

Mark Twain, a celebrated American author renowned for classics like *The Adventures of Tom Sawyer* and *The Adventures of Huckleberry Finn*, imparted timeless wisdom and continues to inspire generations.

BEYOND INTENTIONS: A BLUEPRINT FOR BEHAVIOURAL BREAKTHROUGHS

While the concept of the Strategy Stand-Up might seem straightforward, its power lies in underlying psychological principles. It taps into the human need for accountability, structure and positive reinforcement.

To truly harness the power of the Strategy Stand-Up and turn aspirations into achievements, we must navigate two common behavioural challenges:

1. **Embracing Change:** Recognizing the need for a new behaviour is one thing, but truly integrating it into our routine is another. It's the difference between buying gym shoes and actually using them.

2. **Maintaining Consistency:** Starting is easy; consistency is hard. It's the challenge of keeping up with your gym routine, not just in January but all year round.

NEW BEHAVIOURS

When it comes to Key Activities, there's an undeniable truth: the most transformative tasks are often those we shy away from. These are the endeavours that challenge us, that demand we think bigger and step outside our comfort zones. Yet, in the hustle of daily life, we gravitate toward the familiar and immediate, sidelining what results in positive change.

Consider a team, ignited with ambition at a January strategy session. They've mapped out their goals, charted the course with Key Activities, and are ready to charge ahead. But once they're back in the trenches of daily operations, old habits creep in, overshadowing those grand plans. It's a phenomenon gyms bank on every year. They oversell memberships, knowing full well that many will fall back into old patterns, leaving treadmills empty despite the best of New Year intentions.

The Strategy Stand-Up is designed to cut through that noise, ensuring we're not mistaking motion for progress. In today's world, it's all too easy to confuse busyness with productivity. We're swamped, juggling tasks, putting out fires and drowning in notifications. But amid this chaos, we must ask: are we actually advancing toward our goals?

The Strategy Stand-Up is our compass, ensuring we don't just move, but move in the right direction. It zeroes in on your team's MIGs and the vital Key Activities that drive them. It's not just a checkpoint; it's a recalibration, pulling everyone back to the core mission when daily distractions threaten to derail. And there's no hiding or sidestepping. It's a transparent space where excuses fade, replaced by a shared dedication to the mission.

The heart of this meeting is the commitment phase, where intentions transform into promises. Here, each member voices their objectives for the upcoming week. This isn't just a statement of intent; it's a concrete, vocalized promise to act.

The power of this commitment is magnified by the collective spirit of the team. United in purpose, team members bolster each other, helping colleagues to break free from entrenched habits and foster new, more impactful ones. This collective dynamic plays a crucial role, both in celebrating past successes and when reflecting on deviations from the plan.

These individual promises ensure that your team as a whole allocates sufficient time to your strategic plan. Throughout the week, these promises serve as gentle nudges, keeping everyone aligned with their commitments. Come the next meeting, each member reflects on their promises, establishing a culture of commitments and reviews, week after week, across all teams.

CONSISTENCY

The hard thing about achieving hard things is that it requires consistency. True commitment means showing up, day after day, week after week. In the same vein, the Strategy Stand-Up shouldn't be an occasional ritual but an organization's steadfast weekly tradition. Think of it as the throttle of your vehicle, but instead of propelling the car, it accelerates your company's strategy forward.

It's perplexing, then, to see how many organizations treat their most pivotal tasks – the ones that drive their goals – as mere items to occasionally check off. These tasks, often decided in annual conferences or planning cycles, usually follow a quarterly review rhythm.

Here's a reality check: Key Activities, given their significance and inherent challenges, demand a tighter feedback loop. A monthly or quarterly check-in? That's too sparse. To make revolutionary strides, these discussions need to be weekly. Otherwise, the pace of progress will be too sluggish to have any real impact.

Amid daily diversions and the inherent human resistance to change, consider the transformative power of this rhythmic practice. What if every team, across every department, convened in this deliberate manner week after week? What if each member held not only themselves but their peers accountable to these pivotal yet challenging Key Activities?

Imagine the ripple effect on an organization's culture. Envision the amplified force behind a strategy when every individual, from the intern to the CEO, shoulders this weekly responsibility. The profound impact of fostering a culture where commitment isn't just expected but celebrated. This is an excellent way to contribute to the Execution Revolution in your own sphere of influence.

"A vision and strategy aren't enough.
The long-term key to success is execution.
Each day. Every day."

– RICHARD M KOVACEVICH

Richard M. Kovacevich, the former CEO of Wells Fargo, is a distinguished leader in the financial sector. Under his guidance, Wells Fargo achieved remarkable success, exemplifying the pivotal role of daily execution in realizing a vision and strategy for long-term prosperity.

THE STRATEGY STAND-UP

WHAT IS THE STRATEGY STAND-UP?
The Strategy Stand-Up is a structured, weekly gathering designed to drive teams toward their MIGs and Key Activities. It's not just another meeting; it's a powerful tool that leaders use to:
- Direct the team's efforts toward priority tasks.
- Personally, and openly commit to progress.
- Monitor progress and address any roadblocks.
- Celebrate successes and reinforce the team's purpose.
- Ensure everyone is aligned and accountable.

WHY IS IT EFFECTIVE?
Focus on What Matters: The meeting zeroes in on the team's MIGs and Key Activities, ensuring everyone remains aligned with the overarching objectives, even amid the daily whirlwind of tasks.

Commitment and Accountability: Every member proactively commits to their tasks for the upcoming week. Besides being a professional commitment; it's also a personal one. No one wants to let their team down, so this is a culture where everyone's contribution is visible and valued.

Visualization: By clearly visualizing progress, teams know exactly where to focus. Leaders can preemptively address issues, ensuring smooth execution.

Consistent Cadence: Held weekly, these meetings ensure that teams maintain momentum. Quarterly reviews might lead to complacency, but a weekly check-in keeps everyone on their toes, proactive and engaged.

Engagement and Culture: The Strategy Stand-Up isn't just about tasks; it's about people. Celebrating successes, supporting each other and committing as a team creates a winning culture.

A GUIDE TO FOCUSED EXECUTION

Come Prepared: Leaders should update and reflect on goals, review the past week's results and know the status of Key Activities. Anticipate issues; without preparation, unexpected performance issues might slip through during the Strategy Stand-Up.

Stick to the Structured Agenda: The Strategy Stand-Up is succinct, usually only 15-30 minutes. To ensure focus and efficiency, adhere to the following sequence:

- **Purpose and Progress:** The leader begins by reiterating the significance of the goals and the team's advancement toward them, ensuring the shared 'why' remains front and centre. Following this, the team assesses its trajectory toward these goals. Are our Key Activities yielding the desired results, or is there room for refinement? Regularly revisiting and emphasizing the importance of these goals ensures sustained team alignment and motivation.

- **Commitment Review:** Revisit the pledges made during the previous week. Were they fulfilled as anticipated? This segment often creates constructive peer-driven motivation. Everyone is on a shared journey, collectively pushing boundaries. As a result, the leader is relieved from always playing the role of the 'enforcer.'

- **Share Insights and Hurdles:** Discuss new insights and identify any challenges hindering progress. Celebrate the week's achievements and reflect on any missteps, using them as opportunities for growth.
- **Commitments for the Upcoming Week:** Each member should communicate their specific goals for the next week. It's essential that these commitments represent a clear deliverable. Vague intentions like 'focus on' or 'work on' are insufficient. Such vague commitments, lacking clear outcomes, can easily be forgotten as everyday tasks pop up.

By vocalizing their goals for the coming week, each member reinforces their commitment. It's crucial that team members set their own goals, because this ensures personal ownership. Moreover, these commitments should be transparent within the team, encouraging a culture of collective success.

The leader's role in noting down these commitments is pivotal. By visualizing them in the subsequent meeting, the team can readily assess whether the intended progress was achieved. This routine not only bolsters accountability but also guarantees that Key Activities remain at the forefront of everyone's agenda, driving accountability.

NAVIGATING CHANGE RESISTANCE

In the muted ambience of her digital workspace, Jessica waited for the familiar digital avatars of her Scandinavian team leaders. Her thoughts weighed heavily on her; she had a nagging feeling that something was amiss. While other teams had taken to the new way of working like ducks to water, her Swedish and Norwegian teams seemed to be floundering, their wings clipped by resistance.

She sighed, tapping a rhythm on her desk. The numbers didn't lie. Other teams had embraced their new Key Activities with an enthusiasm that was noticeably absent in her Scandinavian teams. As the minutes ticked by, waiting for Hugo and Erika to join the call, Jessica's resolve hardened. It was time to face the music.

Hugo, with his rugged individualism, was the embodiment of the old-school sales manager, a maverick who played by his own rules. His drive was undeniable, but his reluctance to embrace change was equally evident. Jessica had often admired his spirit, but today, his resistance was causing problems.

Erika was an enigma. From the moment the Swedish affiliate was acquired, a palpable tension surrounded her. Jessica vividly remembered the stormy look in Erika's eyes when she got the news of her demotion, a direct result of the acquisition. While some of Erika's methods were praiseworthy, the scars of her past loomed large, often overshadowing her current contributions. Jessica was well-aware of Erika's fondness for hosting team building sessions. It was a charming touch, but Jessica couldn't help but wonder: was that all there was to Erika's leadership?

As the call connected, Jessica took a deep breath – it was time for some candid conversations. The story of the Scandinavian teams was about to take a new turn, and Jessica was determined to be the author of that change.

With her fingers lightly tapping the edge of her coffee mug, Jessica began. "Hugo, Erika," she said, her voice steady, "I've been reviewing the progress of our European teams, and I've noticed a trend. Many of them are finding significant success with the Strategy Stand-Ups and their Key Activities, translating into tangible results. They're achieving wins that, frankly, we're missing out on here in Scandinavia."

Hugo shifted in his seat, looking slightly defensive. "Jessica, I know you feel these meetings are crucial. But my calendar has been packed. Between my client engagements and follow-ups, it's been a whirlwind."

Jessica raised an eyebrow, her tone firm yet understanding. "Hugo, while I appreciate your dedication to your own sales, your primary role is to ensure your team excels, not just you. These meetings aren't just another task on your calendar. They're our chosen path to ensure we're not just busy, but effective. If other leaders, under similar pressures, can prioritize them, so can we. It's about setting the right example, especially when things are hectic."

Hugo sighed, not very happy with the pushback from Jessica. Hugo valued his autonomy over all else. He tried once more. "Okay, Jess, while I see your point, the reality is that I have two huge tenders out, potentially critically impacting our sales and you know how those templates are to fill in."

Jessica, with a determined glint in her eyes, responded, "Hugo, I completely understand the demands of those templates. But while you're buried in paperwork, your team is navigating without their captain. Remember our strategy discussions? You were right there with us, shaping the vision. It wasn't about perpetuating the cycle of chasing price-driven tenders. It was about evolving and aiming higher."

She paused for a moment, letting her words sink in. "I'm not questioning your dedication, Hugo. But it's essential to ask: are you and your team channelling your energy in the right direction? The Strategy Stand-Ups are our gas-pedal, guiding us toward the behaviours we earmarked in our Key Activities. It's about elevating our conversations, engaging with more senior decision makers, and unlocking multi-business opportunities. Other teams are already reaping the rewards, and we're lagging behind. Can you see the gap I'm pointing out?"

Hugo's shoulders slumped, his face reflecting a moment of clarity. "Jessica," he began, sounding subdued, "I see where you're coming from. Maybe I've been too set in my old ways and hesitant to adapt. Are other teams really finding success with this approach?"

Jessica, recognizing the shift in Hugo's stance, replied directly, "Yes, they are, Hugo. I think it would benefit you to have a discussion with your counterparts in France or Germany. They're implementing the approach effectively and seeing positive outcomes."

Hugo nodded in agreement with Jessica, committing to prioritize the Strategy Stand-Ups from the upcoming Monday. "I'll also reach out to some of my peers," he added, "to understand their tactics and find out how they've successfully integrated these meetings into their teams."

Jessica's attention shifted to Erika, her voice carrying a mix of concern and firmness. "Erika, I've felt a certain hesitance from you. Can you share your thoughts?"

Erika paused, her eyes momentarily avoiding Jessica's. "Jessica, it's not that I'm against the idea. It's just ... I'm not sure if this new approach is the right fit for our team's dynamics."

Jessica, a little taken aback by Erika's candidness, responded thoughtfully. "Could you specify what aspect of the approach feels misaligned? Is it the structure of the meetings, the commitments or something else?" Internally, Jessica couldn't help but wonder if the real resistance was stemming from Erika's personal apprehensions. She remembered Erika's past struggles with change, which had played a part in her demotion three years ago.

Erika fidgeted, clearly uneasy. "I just think our team has a unique rhythm, and I'm concerned this might disrupt it."

Jessica leaned forward and carried on speaking. "Every team has its rhythm, Erika. But as leaders, our role is to evolve that rhythm when needed, making sure it aligns with the broader organizational goals. The Strategy Stand-Ups aren't just a new task; they're a tool to elevate our performance. If other teams, each with their own dynamics, are benefiting, shouldn't we give it a shot?"

Erika took a deep breath, her unease palpable. "Jessica, I understand the direction we're headed in. But my team has always had a tough time with transitions. I sense they won't be too receptive."

Jessica, sensing the need for a firmer stance, took a moment before responding. It was important that her words carried weight. "Erika, it's not about what we've always done. It's about what we can do better. Your role isn't just to manage but to lead, especially through change. Pointing out differences or placing blame elsewhere won't help. I've seen you navigate challenges before. I believe in your ability to lead your team through this. But you need to believe in it too. Can we find a way together to get your team on board? When we introduced this to your team, they seemed open. What's shifted since then?"

Erika hesitated, choosing her words carefully. "In our one-on-ones, many voiced concerns. They have questions, uncertainties."

Jessica, not missing a beat, asked, "And how have you been addressing their concerns during these sessions?"

Erika looked down, "I've been lending an ear, offering support where I can. But I admit, I'm also navigating this new terrain. Some team members feel the public commitments are a form of micromanagement. They've shared with me that it feels like there's a lack of trust from the top."

Jessica chose her words carefully. "Erika, let's talk openly for a moment. We've gone over the rationale behind our methods multiple times. The strategic importance of our goals, the pressing business imperatives of our initiatives, and the essence of the Strategy Stand-Up have all been laid out. But just being the messenger between your team and the higher-ups isn't really leading, is it? Leadership isn't just about being everyone's friend. Sometimes, it's about facing those tough conversations head-on."

With a gentler tone, she continued, "Erika, I sense that the team's hesitancy might be mirroring your own doubts. If they see that fire in your eyes, that unwavering belief in our direction, they'll rally behind you. And remember, you're not alone in this." Her voice softened, "What if I join you for the next Strategy Stand-Up? A united front might be just what we need to steer the ship through stormy waters."

Erika shifted in her seat, her eyes darting away for a moment. The weight of the situation pressed on her, and her voice trembled slightly as she responded, "I appreciate that, Jessica. But you should know, we didn't set any commitments last time. There's ... resistance, and I've tried to keep things fluid to avoid getting stuck in endless debates. Our end game is the clients, right?"

"Absolutely, Erika. But it's about connecting with the right clients, with purpose and strategy." She gave a reassuring nod, her voice steady and supportive. "On Monday, let's face this together. And afterwards, we'll meet for a debrief."

> *"Change is hard because people overestimate the value of what they have and underestimate the value of what they may gain by giving that up."*
>
> **- JAMES A. BELASCO & RALPH STAYER**

James A. Belasco and Ralph Stayer are authors and thought leaders in organizational development. Their work, including the book *Flight of the Buffalo: Soaring to Excellence, Learning to Let Employees Lead,* has provided valuable insights into change management and leadership, guiding organizations toward embracing change and empowering employees

THE RISKS WHEN AUTONOMY OVERSHADOWS ACCOUNTABILITY

While organizations stand to achieve significant advancements by adopting the strategies outlined in this book, the crux of successful implementation also rests on the shoulders of individual leaders. Their ability to steer difficult dialogues, much like Jessica's interaction with her Scandinavian team, is paramount. It involves directly addressing those wrestling with change, revisiting discussions to ensure clarity, and securing unequivocal commitments.

"The challenge of leadership is to be strong, but not rude; be kind, but not weak; be bold, but not a bully; be thoughtful, but not lazy; be humble, but not timid; be proud, but not arrogant; have humour, but without folly."

– JIM ROHN

Jim Rohn, a well-known personal development philosopher, has made significant contributions to leadership and personal growth. With a legacy spanning decades, he shared timeless wisdom and insights through his speeches, books and seminars. Some of his most notable works include *The Challenge to Succeed* and *Five Major Pieces to the Life Puzzle*.

In the following sections, we will look closely at common resistance behaviours, identify signs of such behaviours, and provide guidance on how leaders can effectively address and navigate them.

THE AUTONOMY ILLUSIONISTS

The Autonomy Illusionists are those leaders who ardently believe that autonomy is the medicine for all organizational challenges. They operate under the conviction that any form of oversight or management from above is a direct threat to team engagement and productivity. They can often be recognized by their strong advocacy for complete independence and their resistance to any top-down directives or strategies.

The core belief driving this behaviour is the notion that those closest to the work should be the primary decision makers. By granting teams full autonomy, the illusionists believe they are creating an environment where individuals can operate at their peak efficiency, free from the interruptions and constraints of 'management.'

While such an approach can indeed boost engagement and a sense of ownership, especially during prosperous times, it falters during periods of change or uncertainty. The Autonomy Illusionists often underestimate the need for direction and leadership, especially in rough seas. They excel when the going is good but can become paralysed or ineffective when change is on the horizon. Their teams, while enjoying autonomy, can often feel rudderless when a clear direction or decision is needed.

Leaders encountering Autonomy Illusionists in their ranks must strike a delicate balance. It's essential to remind these individuals of their pivotal role in guiding and leading their teams, especially during transformative phases. While autonomy is valuable, it shouldn't eclipse accountability.

Leaders should encourage the Autonomy Illusionists to find a middle ground between granting independence and ensuring alignment with organizational goals.

Instead of issuing directives, help them craft a narrative where change isn't imposed but co-created. Engage them in facilitating team discussions to collaboratively chart the new course. Often, the resistance isn't against accountability but against feeling sidelined in decision making. By involving them in shaping the direction, you address their core concern while prioritizing timely and effective execution.

THE CONSENSUS CHASERS

The Consensus Chasers, at first glance, might seem similar to the Autonomy Illusionists, but their motivations are very different. These leaders have an aversion to discomfort and conflict, often stemming from a deep-seated desire for camaraderie and harmony within their teams. Recognizable by their frequent references to team sentiments and their tendency to act as conduits between senior management and their teams, they rarely take personal ownership of change. Instead, they often deflect responsibility, emphasizing that decisions come from above and hoping their teams won't "shoot the messenger." To their superiors, they may come across as perpetual complainers, often attributing their lack of progress to external circumstances.

Rooted in their belief that a leader's success is contingent on being well-liked, they prioritize positive group dynamics. Their leadership style is often heavily influenced by past experiences, especially if they've encountered authoritarian figures in their careers. They believe that a harmonious team, free from interpersonal conflicts or frustrations stemming from management decisions, is more productive. By making sure that any change is thoroughly anchored within the team, they ensure that when action is finally taken, it's backed by robust support.

While their emphasis on consensus can sometimes yield positive results, it mostly leads to overcomplication and delays. Their over-reliance on achieving unanimous agreement means they frequently overspend valuable time that could be better utilized executing strategy. As well as that, their reluctance to address individual underperformance, for fear of causing discomfort, can lead to inefficiencies. In essence, their preference for being liked can sometimes overshadow the need for effective leadership and timely decision making.

It's crucial for these leaders to recognize that leadership, by its very nature, will occasionally involve facing resistance and making unpopular decisions. While consensus is valuable, it shouldn't come at the cost of efficiency. Often, what these leaders need most is assistance in framing the 'why' behind a change. By helping them explain the rationale for change in a manner that resonates with their team, putting it in place becomes easier. When guiding such leaders, it's essential to consistently remind them of the broader objectives and the reasons behind them. This not only aids them in team communication but also reinforces the importance of timely, decisive action.

THE IDLE ENGINE ACCEPTORS

The Idle Engine Acceptors are emblematic of the laid-back, low-engagement managerial style. Their priorities lean heavily toward personal life and outside-of-work activities, often emphasizing a lifestyle-driven approach to their roles. The quintessential 'business as usual' managers, they prioritize work-life balance, with the scales tipping decidedly toward 'life.'

Rooted in the belief that 'slow is smooth, and smooth is fast' (a phrase often attributed to special operations forces emphasizing the importance of deliberate action), these leaders feel that overburdening their teams is detrimental and chaotic. They view excessive stress as one of the primary culprits behind workplace dissatisfaction. Their approach isn't necessarily borne out of malice or negligence toward the company; rather, it's a conscious choice to maintain a consistent pace. Their loyalty to the organization can be unwavering, but it's often on their own terms.

While it's undeniable that stress plays a role in workplace challenges, research indicates that the sheer volume of work isn't the primary stressor. Instead, feelings of powerlessness and the inability to influence one's work environment are more significant contributors to stress. By setting a slower pace as the norm, these leaders inadvertently impose their tempo on their entire team, regardless of individual preferences. This often leads to inefficiencies, with team members waiting on decisions or inputs from these managers. Their tendency to operate at a leisurely pace can inadvertently create bottlenecks, hampering the team's overall productivity.

To effectively manage the Idle Engine Acceptors, it's crucial to strike a balance between respecting their preference for a steady pace and the organization's need for timely results. Begin by setting clear expectations and deadlines, making sure they understand the organization's broader goals. Encourage open communication, allowing them to voice their concerns about potential stressors. Implement regular check-ins to monitor progress and address any potential bottlenecks promptly.

Consider offering training sessions on time management and decision making to help them optimize their workflow. Lastly, foster an environment where team members feel empowered to influence their work conditions, thereby addressing one of the primary causes of workplace stress. By taking these steps, you can help these leaders align their personal preferences with the organization's objectives, promoting a harmonious and productive work environment.

THE SHORT-TERM OPTIMIZERS

Short-term Optimizers are characterized by their laser focus on immediate gains, often at the expense of long-term value. Their mindset is rooted in the desire for instant rewards, making them hesitant to invest time or resources in tasks that don't promise immediate returns, especially if they don't directly influence their short-term bonuses.

Guided by the principle that 'a bird in the hand is worth two in the bush,' these individuals prioritize tangible, immediate benefits over potential future gains. Their approach is methodical, often adhering strictly to established best practices. They believe in the certainty of the present and are wary of the future's unpredictability. By consistently meeting short-term targets, they feel they are contributing effectively to the organization.

While achieving short-term targets is commendable, an overemphasis on immediate gains can hinder strategic growth. Sometimes, companies need to pivot or adopt new strategies that require patience and a willingness to forgo immediate rewards in favour of more significant future benefits. Short-term Optimizers often find it challenging to adapt during these strategic shifts. Their reluctance to take risks or invest in initiatives with delayed payoffs can stifle innovation and limit the organization's potential for growth. Moreover, by focusing solely on immediate rewards, they might miss out on opportunities that could yield substantial benefits in the long run.

When dealing with Short-term Optimizers, it's essential to recognize their loyalty to incentive programs. To harness this loyalty effectively, one should restructure these programs to encompass both immediate and future-oriented goals. Introducing rewards for accomplishing Key Activities and aligning bonuses with the team's MIGs can be beneficial.

These people thrive when they have a lucid grasp of the organization's overarching objectives. By consistently communicating the foundational business logic and long-term vision, and emphasizing the 'why' behind strategic choices, you can guide them to look beyond the allure of immediate rewards and recognize the significance of investments that promise long-term returns.

In essence, while the Short-term Optimizers' focus on immediate results can be an asset in certain scenarios, it's crucial to guide them toward a more balanced perspective that values both short-term achievements and long-term growth.

THE DISTRACTED WHIRLWINDERS

The Distracted Whirlwinders are a unique breed of professionals who, at first glance, appear to be the epitome of productivity. Their desks are a flurry of activity, their calendars packed, and their email inboxes always pinging. However, upon closer inspection, one might notice a pattern of scattered focus and a tendency to jump from one task to another without completing anything.

At the heart of their behaviour is a genuine desire to accomplish everything and meet everyone's expectations. They often believe that multitasking is their superpower. The immediate satisfaction of ticking off smaller tasks or responding to every email as it comes in gives them a sense of accomplishment.

Having a Whirlwinder in your team or organization can be beneficial in situations that require rapid responses or handling of multiple minor tasks simultaneously. Their ability to keep many balls in the air can be impressive, and they often thrive in roles that demand such juggling.

However, the constant, chaotic activity can lead to significant issues in the long run. Important projects requiring deep focus and sustained attention can suffer. They might struggle to see tasks through to completion, leading to a backlog of half-finished projects. Their scattered approach can also lead to missed details, errors and oversights. Over time, the constant state of distraction can lead to burnout, decreased job satisfaction and diminished overall productivity.

Guiding a Distracted Whirlwinder demands a thoughtful approach. While it's essential to acknowledge their energy and enthusiasm, guiding them toward structured and goal-oriented methods is also vital. Leveraging Key Activities and factoring in consistent progress checks during the Strategy Stand-Up can be transformative. This approach aids in segmenting their tasks, preventing them from feeling swamped as deadlines loom. The objective is not to curb their enthusiasm but to harness it in a manner that works for both the individual and the organization.

For those prone to distractions, it is necessary to emphasize the distinction between mere activity and genuine progress. A practical Key Activity for them is 'Time Blocks,' where they allocate specific hours in their calendar exclusively for their Key Activities. This tactic compels the Distracted Whirlwinder to focus on priorities, as concentrated effort is often their challenge. Encourage them to mute all notifications for a couple of hours, allowing undivided attention to a single task. Periodic one-on-one sessions, with Key Activities as the focal point, can offer invaluable support and direction.

THE DEVELOPMENT DODGERS

Development Dodgers are easily recognizable by their reluctance to embrace new tools, techniques or methodologies. These individuals often shy away from opportunities for personal and professional growth, preferring to remain in their comfort zones.

While they may be competent in their current roles, they tend to avoid challenges, new training or any situation that might expose gaps in their knowledge or skills. They might often use phrases like, "This is how we've always done it," or "If it isn't broken, don't fix it." While they may excel in their current tasks, they hesitate to take on new responsibilities or learn new skills, fearing failure or exposure.

While the Development Dodgers' approach might seem safe in the short term, it can be detrimental in the long run. Industries evolve, and so do job roles. By dodging opportunities for growth, they risk becoming obsolete or less valuable to the organization. Their reluctance to adapt can also hinder team progress, especially if the team needs to adopt new strategies or tools.

Engaging with Development Dodgers requires a blend of understanding and motivation. It's essential to recognize the root of their hesitancy. Often, they need tangible evidence that a new method or approach works before they're willing to adopt it. Abstract concepts or theoretical benefits might not resonate with them.

Instead, they value practical demonstrations and real-world results.

To address this, pair them with colleagues who have already embraced newer methods and have seen positive outcomes. These peers, preferably from similar teams handling analogous tasks, can showcase the practicalities and advantages of new processes. Witnessing a peer succeed with a new approach can be far more convincing than any presentation slide. This hands-on, peer-to-peer learning can bridge the gap between reluctance and adoption.

However, if a Development Dodger holds a pivotal role and their resistance impedes organizational progress, more decisive action might be necessary. While it's essential to provide ample opportunities for growth and adaptation, there comes a point where the organization's needs outweigh individual comfort.

In such cases, consider transitioning them to a different role that more closely matches their current skill set. If resistance persists and hampers the team's evolution, it might be in the best interest of both the individual and the organization to consider parting ways. Pushing a Development Dodger too hard or too quickly can lead to significant stress for them. Sometimes, a fresh start, either in a new role or a new organization, can be the most compassionate and practical solution.

STEERING AND STRENGTHENING

As her computer's clock blinked closer to the scheduled time, Jessica readied herself for the Swedish Sales team's Strategy Stand-Up. Before diving in, she decided to review the latest progress reports. A swift analysis of her entire organization confirmed her suspicions: while most of her teams were flourishing, the Scandinavian ones were merely treading water.

Zooming in on the local data, she noticed a lack of commitment to the last few months' Key Activities. It was no surprise that their MIGs were stagnating. A twinge of annoyance hit her. The correlation between effort and outcome was evident. If she were in their shoes, she'd be mortified, especially when comparing their performance to other teams who, under similar circumstances, were achieving remarkable success. But with a leader who seemed so resistant to change, what else could she expect?

Shaking off her frustration, Jessica decided to approach the situation with a more positive mindset, searching for any silver linings in the data. And there it was: Douglas, a relatively new face, had made significant strides in the Stockholm region. She had heard about him a couple of times. A fresh graduate from Lund University, his unconventional approach might be just the breath of fresh air the team needed.

She thought about what she knew about Douglas. His adventurous nature might mean he sees challenges as opportunities rather than obstacles. Jessica allowed herself a hopeful smile. Maybe, just maybe, Douglas could be the catalyst for change the team so desperately needed. She hoped that he would be comfortable becoming somewhat of a poster-boy for what Jessica had planned for the upcoming meeting.

As she logged in to the meeting, she was relieved to see Douglas already among them. His presence would be instrumental to her plans.

"Good morning, everyone!" Erika began. "It's evident to all of us that we've faced challenges with this meeting format, especially since it's been weeks since our last attempt. However, I believe we've made significant strides, albeit in our unique ways," she added, subtly hinting that the team wasn't neglecting their strategy. Yet, Jessica's recent data analysis suggested otherwise.

"Let's quickly review last week's activities." Erika continued as team members began sharing their updates, Jessica discerned a recurring theme: a heavy focus on routine tasks. Moreover, the updates varied wildly. Some delved deep into details, recounting almost every action from the past week, while others provided only a cursory overview. By the time the fifth member embarked on an exhaustive rundown, Jessica's patience had worn thin. She was there to effect change, not to listen to a drawn-out chronicle of the week.

"I apologize for cutting in during your recap," Jessica interrupted the flow, "but I've observed there's little mention of our strategic direction, your team's MIGs and crucially, the Key Activities. My primary reason for joining today is to gauge our progress and understand any challenges you might be facing. Could we perhaps concentrate on that during this call? If there's a need for a more routine update, maybe it can be addressed after we wrap up?"

Jessica continued in her gentle tone, "Could you perhaps share any advancements you made last week concerning your Key Activities?" She sensed the discomfort of the young sales rep from Northern Sweden, who was momentarily caught off guard. His eyes darted to Erika, seeking guidance.

Erika, sensing his unease, stepped in. "Before your input, Jessica, Jonas was discussing his involvement in several tenders and price negotiations with some of our major clients. We had decided that would be his primary focus last week, so he didn't take on any new Key Activities."

Jessica took a deep breath, her gaze flitting between the faces on the screen. She was wary of undermining Erika, the local team leader. But given Erika's recent attempt to side with the team's perspective, Jessica felt compelled to step in and make her point. "Understood," she responded, her voice firm yet measured. She realized they could either engage in a prolonged, awkward exchange or address the matter directly, even if it stung a bit. Opting for the latter, she took control of the meeting from Erika. Sharing her screen, she accessed their strategy execution platform and swiftly navigated to the team's page.

Jessica began to address the team. "When I review your dashboard, tracing actions back to the top priorities, a few things become clear," she started, her words chosen with care. "You've identified two MIGs – the ones that should matter more than any other goals, guiding your actions above all else. The first MIG revolves around total new sales, measured in contract value. While we're not exactly setting the world on fire with it, you're making decent progress. The second, however, is about expanding our revenue from our top clients by introducing them to more of our business lines. This goal aligns with the Strategic Initiative 'Expansion,' echoing its significance to our company's future trajectory. And yet, it's trailing behind."

She paused, allowing the room a moment to reflect. "This brings us to a pivotal juncture. Either the perception of what's most important has shifted in the past few months, which means we need a fresh discussion on priorities, or we've simply not been laser-focused on this goal."

Jessica's demeanour softened, her eyes scanning the faces on the screen. "I understand the challenges of engaging with senior stakeholders. I've had numerous dialogues across Europe on this very topic. Your concerns, your hesitations – I've encountered them all.

"But here's a broader perspective. In Germany, they're outperforming you by a massive 500% on this MIG. France is at 450%, and both the Netherlands and Spain are at 300%." With practiced ease, she showcased the achievements of the other teams on the strategy software. "The secret isn't in market nuances or product differences. It's their unwavering commitment to their Key Activities. They've amplified their efforts, and the results are evident. This isn't mere speculation any more; it's a proven strategy."

Her eyes found Douglas, a hint of a smile playing on her lips. "Speaking of amplified efforts, Douglas here has been making significant strides in your local market. He's leading the charge, showing us what's possible. Douglas, would you care to share some of your insights?"

Douglas looked momentarily taken aback, clearly not expecting to be thrust into the limelight. He shifted in his seat, a brief flash of unease crossing his face. But as the meaning of Jessica's words settled in, his posture relaxed, and a youthful grin spread across his face.

"Whoa, Jessica," he began with a light chuckle, "Didn't see that coming. Kinda feels like being called out in class, doesn't it?" He scratched the back of his head, searching for the right words. "So, yeah, when I was over in the States for my master's, I kinda got roped into this sales team. We were, like, dabbling with this whole strategic sales approach, you know? Did some groundwork, had some chats with the big shots, and it just ... clicked for me."

He paused, his eyes darting around as he gathered his scattered thoughts. "I mean, getting these top-tier folks on the line? Not gonna lie, it's a bit of a hustle. But once you're in, it's a whole different ball game. They're chill, open to bigger deals, and there's way less of that cutthroat vibe.

"Hearing about the wins in Germany and France and all? Totally tracks. This stuff's legit. And, well, I just thought, why not give it a shot here? Seems to be working out, right?" He ended with a sheepish shrug, his casual demeanour a stark contrast to the room's earlier intensity.

"Douglas, would you be up for hosting a session later this week?" Jessica inquired, her tone both hopeful and challenging.

"I'm thinking you could share your approach with the team, especially those who haven't tried this method yet. Maybe walk them through your phone pitch and any other insights on securing those meetings?"

Douglas's eyes widened a fraction as Jessica's proposal registered. "You want me to run a session?" he asked, a mix of surprise and excitement evident in his voice.

But as the weight of the recognition from the higher-ups settled in, his initial shock transformed into pride. "Yeah, sure thing, Jessica. I can totally whip up something for the team." He paused, a determined glint in his eyes. "I'll make sure it's top-notch, promise." He mentally committed to burning the midnight oil, making sure his presentation would be nothing short of stellar. After all, with the big boss taking notice, this was his chance to shine and potentially fast-track his career.

Jessica, sensing the shift in the room's energy, turned her attention back to the team. "I can't stress enough how vital this approach is for our success. I urge everyone here, especially if you're still on the fence about this strategy, to attend Douglas's session. If you can't make it, catch up with him later. We've seen the results; we know it's a game-changer. I'd like each of you to dedicate some time this week to identify potential stakeholders within your major accounts. By next week, I expect to see commitments to this Key Activity.

"Erika and I had some preliminary discussions about this direction before today's meeting," Jessica said, subtly emphasizing their shared leadership. "Based on our conversations and today's insights, do you feel this aligns with the vision we've been crafting together for the team?" Jessica was deliberate in her approach.

While she may have stretched the truth regarding the depth of their prior agreement, she felt it was necessary. Earlier in the meeting, Erika seemed to side with the team's myriad of excuses, which Jessica viewed as slight disloyalty. Now, she aimed to position Erika as an equal stakeholder in the team's future direction, ensuring her continued significance in the decision-making process.

Erika's response caught Jessica off guard. "Jessica, I'm grateful you joined us today. It's enlightening to hear about the successes of other teams, and Douglas, your initiative is commendable. You've set a brilliant example for all of us. Here's my proposal: this week, let's each identify at least five stakeholders we aim to engage. Bring these names to Douglas's workshop so we have a tangible starting point. Next week, we'll shift our focus back to our Key Activity – securing those crucial meetings. I also recommend turning Thursday's training into a regular session. We'll benefit from ongoing support and shared experiences. Thoughts, everyone?"

A THOUGHTFUL DEBRIEF

The screen blinked to grey as the team meeting ended, leaving Jessica alone with her thoughts. She took a deep breath, her fingers drumming lightly on the desk. In moments like these, the weight of leadership settled on her shoulders – a weight she welcomed but never underestimated.

In a few minutes, Erika would join her for their one-on-one debrief. Jessica knew this conversation needed a different approach. The group meeting was about steering the ship; this was about guiding the captain.

The screen flickered again, and Erika's face appeared, a little pale and strained. Jessica greeted her with a warm, albeit professional, smile. "Erika, thank you for joining me. I hope you're feeling alright after our full-team session."

Erika offered a small, somewhat tentative smile in return. "Jessica, it's good to see you. And yes, I'm ... well, I'm here. Ready to talk."

Jessica nodded, her tone softening. "I appreciate your openness, Erika. It seemed like there was more on your mind during the meeting. Let's use this time to talk freely, just between us. What's on your mind?"

Taking a deep breath, Erika's eyes shone with a mix of fear and resolve. "I've always been worried about letting people down, especially after a couple of tough spots in the past. But what you did today, how you handled things ... it's made me see things differently."

Jessica leaned in, her voice steady and reassuring. "We all have those fears, Erika. But it's what we do with them that counts. Being a leader isn't about being perfect. What's the biggest thing that's holding you back right now?"

As Erika opened up about her past struggles, her voice began to steady, a sign of her growing confidence. "You know, lately I've been hesitant of driving change. Especially whenever there is friction from my team. I don't know. I haven't the best track record for making the right bets, and I guess not making bets seems less daunting."

Jessica's tone was gentle, yet firm. "We've all got things in our past we wish we could change, Erika." Gradually, Erika sat up straighter, as if Jessica's words were physically lightening her load. "I never really thought about it like that. I've been so worried about getting it wrong, I haven't been taking the chances I should."

"That's a good realization," Jessica encouraged. "What's one thing you can do to start taking those chances?"

Erika's face lit up with a tentative hope. "There's Douglas's workshop next week. I could really get behind it, show the team it's okay to step out of our comfort zone."

Jessica's smile was warm and approving. "That's a great first step. And remember, being brave doesn't mean you aren't afraid. It means you go ahead even when you are. And you're not doing this alone – I'm right here with you."

The call ended not just with a list of action items, but with a shared vision that was stronger for its foundation in mutual understanding and respect. As the screen went dark, Jessica felt a quiet confidence in Erika's abilities. And Erika, for her part, felt something she hadn't in a long time – a spark of excitement about the leader she was becoming, fuelled by the realization that vulnerability, paired with action, was a powerful form of courage.

A CULTURE OF COMMITMENT

Forget the drawn-out transformation projects that fade away, the initiatives that fall flat, and the distrust that shadows many corporate hallways. Instead, picture a vibrant workplace where everyone is all in. They're accepting deadlines and committing to outcomes. And every week, they're held accountable, leading to a turbocharged strategy and skyrocketing results.

WHY DOES THIS MATTER SO MUCH?

It's about focus. It's about ensuring that the big things – the things that really move the needle – don't get lost in the daily shuffle. For teams, it's a road map, a clear path forward. Everyone's on board, everyone understands the 'why' and everyone's invested. Individuals? They come prepared, ready to dive in and eager to make a difference.

High-commitment teams are a breed apart. They don't just do the work; they go the extra mile. They're not about excuses; they're about excellence. We've all seen teams that just go through the motions. But in a culture of commitment, there's a drive that's hard to miss.

This isn't just about ticking boxes or nodding to the boss. It's a promise – a promise to peers, to the company and to oneself. It's taking charge of calendars, tackling the tough stuff head-on, and making sure the big priorities are front and centre. It's making promises and keeping them, week in and week out. It's the secret sauce that propels organizations to new heights, turning goals into realities.

CHAPTER 7

THE STRATEGY ORPHAN AND TREATING PLANNING AS SOMEONE ELSE'S PROBLEM

In a world not so different from ours, there exists a peculiar institution known as the Strategy Orphanage. Here, strategies, once brimming with potential and promise, are left abandoned by managers who deemed them too cumbersome or inconvenient. These orphaned strategies wander the halls, hoping for a kind soul to adopt them and nurture them to fruition.

Busy managers, in their haste and hubris, drop off their strategy-children at the orphanage's doorstep, believing that someone else will come along to raise them. And so, the orphanage becomes crowded, its corridors echoing with the sounds of strategies yearning to be realized, while the manager-parents leave, busy being busy.

*"Strategy execution isn't something other
people should worry about while you are
doing something far more important."*

– JEROEN DE FLANDER

Jeroen de Flander, a leading expert in strategy execution, is the author of several acclaimed books, including *The Execution Shortcut* and *The Art of Performance*, which have provided invaluable insights for organizations worldwide.
He is a sought-after advisor and speaker on strategy execution.

From this peculiar place, we transition to a more
grounded reality that demands dedication, understanding and, most importantly, action. But in the relentless
rhythm of business, where calendars dictate actions
and urgencies overshadow importance, strategies often
become overlooked.

The managerial culture often emphasizes the importance of delegation, viewing it as a hallmark of effective
management. However, the boundary between effective
delegation and outright abdication is a fine one, and it's
all too easy to cross. Senior managers frequently lay out
the broad strokes of a strategy and then, perhaps feeling
their job is done, step back, leaving the intricate details
to their teams. This approach has its pitfalls.

One major oversight is the lack of emphasis on strategic planning education. Many managers aren't perceived
as strategic, not due to a lack of capability, but because
they've never been trained to think and act strategically.
Research indicates that a staggering 90% of directors
and vice presidents have never received training to hone
their skills as competent business strategists.[8] This gap
in knowledge becomes evident when these managers
are presented with detailed plans.

Pressed for time, senior managers might only give these plans a cursory glance, missing out on the intricate details and, more critically, the essence of the strategy. This superficial approach leaves them unaware of the strategic choices and nuances embedded within the plans. Consequently, there's a prevailing tendency to settle for what's 'good' rather than striving for what's 'great,' which will become a significant impediment to realizing the full potential of a strategy.

However, this chapter is not a lamentation of what's amiss but a journey toward what can be. We'll go beyond the pitfalls, exploring robust governance structures that seamlessly integrate into management teams, enhancing planning quality while optimizing time. The emphasis will be on the art of crafting milestones, those pivotal markers that transform a strategy from a mere vision to a tangible road map without drowning managers in detail.

In the dynamic dance of business, where change is the only constant, we'll focus on the delicate balance of commitment and adaptability. A meticulously designed yearly cycle is the answer, blending the steadfastness of strategic intent with the agility to adapt, ensuring that strategies remain relevant and resonant.

OPERATIVE MINDSET
FOR STRATEGY

In previous discussions, we delved into planning from the perspective of individual teams, particularly focusing on Key Activities. We touched upon the transformative power of planning one initiative at a time and the essence of reverse-engineered planning. Now, we're elevating this discussion to encompass governance structures for strategic planning, emphasizing the importance of maintaining a consistent planning rhythm throughout the year.

Many senior managers, in their day-to-day roles, don't actively engage with the operational facets of strategy. They're either swamped with decision making or grappling with unresolved issues. It's infrequent for them, or their teams, to truly connect with the strategy, to actively shape it, refine its direction, and champion its execution. It's not about micromanaging the details, but rather about being hands-on, understanding its pulse, and ensuring it's alive and thriving in the organization. The operational whirlwind, it seems, is too overpowering.

However, this approach is counterproductive. Senior leaders should be at the forefront of strategic tasks, investing in today for a better tomorrow. A series of compelling time-studies by the Economist Intelligence Unit,[9] *Harvard Business Review*,[10] and the Strategic Thinking Institute[11] sought to understand the relationship between time spent on strategy and financial performance. They categorized companies into top financial performers and the rest, analysing the time dedicated to strategy across different levels of seniority.

Here's what they found:

- In an average company, the C-suite dedicates 10% of their time to strategic tasks, roughly four hours

weekly per executive. However, this strategic focus
lessens down the hierarchy, with managers allocating
under 5% and regular employees a mere 1%

- Contrast this with top financial performers: the
  C-suite spend 30% of their time on strategy, managers
  contribute 15% and, notably, regular employees
  allocate 10% of their time toward strategic goals.

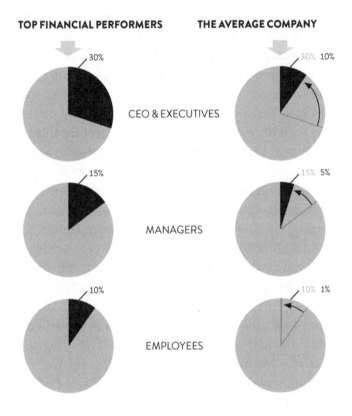

TOP FINANCIAL PERFORMERS   **THE AVERAGE COMPANY**

30%   30% 10%

CEO & EXECUTIVES

15%   15% 5%

MANAGERS

10%   10% 1%

EMPLOYEES

To grasp the real-world implications of these findings, consider a hypothetical company of 300 employees. In such a setting, top-performing companies
would have their management team invest 72 hours

weekly on strategy, compared to 24 hours by their average counterparts. With 30 managers, top performers would dedicate 240 hours, while the average company would only manage 60 hours. The most striking difference emerges at the employee level: 1,200 hours from top performers versus a mere 120 hours from the average company.

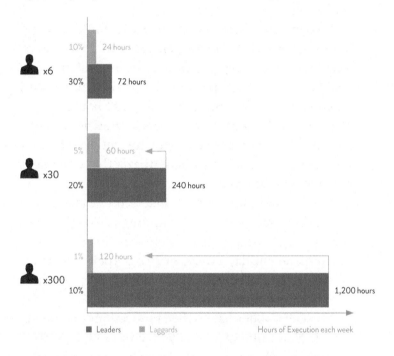

The disparity isn't just a matter of numbers; it's a profound divide in organizational commitment and momentum. Consider the difference: top performers channelling 1,500 hours each week toward strategic objectives, while the average company allocates just 200 hours. This isn't a slight variation; it's a contrast between an organization pulsating with strategic dynamism, innovation and progress, versus one that's merely going through the motions. This is the Execution Revolution in numbers. And the results speak for themselves. The top financial performers, those who prioritize strategy, not only grow at a rate 40% faster but also boast a profitability margin that's 52% higher than their counterparts.[8] These aren't just statistics; they're compelling reasons for leaders to prioritize time and actively engage.

Imagine the sheer volume of ideas, initiatives and improvements that can be generated in 1,500 hours, weekly. It's like having a dedicated army of thinkers and doers, relentlessly pushing the organization toward its strategic north star. In contrast, 200 hours, spread across an entire organization, barely scratches the surface. It's the difference between a torrential downpour nourishing the land and a light drizzle that evaporates before it hits the ground.

A real-world example that underscores the power of dedicating time to strategic thinking is Google's '20% time' policy. This initiative encourages Google employees to spend one day a week, or 20% of their work time, on projects they're passionate about, even if these aren't directly related to their operational, day-to-day tasks. Such a policy has birthed innovations like Gmail, Google News and AdSense. By carving out for strategic endeavours, Google not only drives innovation but also aligns its workforce with a broader strategic vision.

Now, a cheeky challenge for you: open up your calendar from last week. Go through each entry and tally up the hours you genuinely spent on proactive strategic tasks. How many hours did you dedicate to shaping the future of your organization? Where do you stand in this spectrum? Are you part of the torrent or the drizzle?

This exercise isn't just about self-reflection; it's a call to action. The data is clear: for an organization to thrive, commitment to strategy must be unwavering, and it must start at the very top. The C-suite's dedication is a powerful signal, a beacon that guides and galvanizes the entire organization.

Embracing an operative mindset for strategy translates to setting aside about 1.5 proactive days in your week, consistently. This is the time you'll use to actively plan your Strategic Initiatives and Key Activities for your team, execute your own Key Activities, communicate the 'Why,' champion the cause within your organization, monitor your team's progress, and address any challenges or resistance that might emerge. While 70% of your time will still be dedicated to day-to-day responsibilities, don't underestimate the immense value that stems from the 30% allocated to strategy.

THE REAL TIME SAVER

Managing your strategy can feel like a mountain to climb. But here's the truth: it's not about adding more to your plate. It's about choosing the right tasks and executing them flawlessly. By proactively honing in on the most impactful tasks, leaders can achieve more, reduce their workload and steer clear of unexpected crises. This isn't just a comforting notion; it's a fact backed by solid research.

Over two years, researcher Simon Elvnäs conducted a detailed time study of more than 400 managers and found a significant insight: up to 50% of a leader's time is spent on redoing tasks that weren't done right the first time.[12] This includes fixing errors, reactively context switching, and adjusting the tactics employed by their teams, simply because they weren't dealt with effectively from the outset.

The core message of this book is straightforward: by taking a proactive approach from the beginning, most repetitive tasks can be eliminated. A lot of them crop up due to a lack of clear direction and initiative, and a lack of great commitment and feedback cycles. By adopting the methodologies outlined here, leaders stand to transform their work experience.

When teams are fully engaged, proactive and aligned with the organization's strategic objectives, leaders find themselves free from incessant distractions. This freedom allows them to steer the organization toward its future, rather than being anchored by the challenges of the past.

Next, we'll focus on the best practices for organizing meetings throughout the year. The aim is to ensure that leaders not only meet their strategic goals but also find the process streamlined and straightforward. We'll discuss the essential steering forums, determine their optimal frequency, design effective agendas, and offer guidance on seamlessly integrating these into daily operations.

CORPORATE EVOLUTION

The CEO entered the room, his demeanour noticeably lighter than usual. There was a certain optimistic energy about him. "Welcome," he began, with a genuine smile. "Today's session is one I've been looking forward to. You know, on and off for the past couple of months, I've been reflecting on a particular quote that I'd like to discuss.

"If the lessons of history teach us anything, it's that nobody learns the lessons that history teaches us." He looked around the room, gauging reactions. "It's a thought-provoking statement. But considering our progress over the past nine months, I'd argue that we're an exception. We've evolved, haven't we?"

"I've been here long enough to see many of the company's phases. And I must say, this feels different. We're not just going through the motions any more," Margaret agreed.

"When I first stepped into my role," Fiona reflected, "there was a worrying sense of uncertainty. Many were questioning the direction we were taking, and there were whispers and doubts about the decisions coming from this very room. But over time, as we started implementing our strategies and seeing the results, those murmurs began to fade. The teams started to see the bigger picture and the vision we were all working toward. And if you want evidence," she paused, raising an eyebrow with a hint of challenge, "have you seen the latest employee satisfaction numbers?"

Alex's eyes lit up, recognizing the cue. "Seen it? Oh, I've been living it!" he exclaimed, his voice filled with pride. "It's been a whirlwind, no doubt. My calendar's been packed – meetings, brainstorming sessions, late-night calls. But what my calendar doesn't show is the sense of purpose that drove us."

He continued, "Sure, there were challenges. Anytime you're charting new territory, there will be. But you know, every time we hit a snag, we learned something. And when people pushed back, we got clearer on our game plan. Supporting our managers, ensuring everyone was on board – it all required effort, but it was the kind of effort that reminds you of why you're passionate about what you do."

His eyes sparkled with pride, "And now, seeing where we are, feeling the shift in our teams – it's rewarding. The numbers are a testament to our collective effort, and the renewed energy in our teams speaks volumes."

With a light-hearted nudge toward their CFO, Richard, he added, "Come on, Dick, even with your keen eye for detail, you've got to appreciate the strides we've made, right?"

"I won't deny the progress," Richard began. "The numbers have improved, and that's commendable. But," he paused, choosing his words carefully, "we've also got to be honest about where we fell short. Some of our initiatives? They didn't hit the mark we aimed for. We need to understand why and adjust. I'm not being pessimistic; I just want to make sure we're always moving in the right direction."

The CEO felt hugely grateful for his team and their efforts. "I appreciate the energy and dedication each of you brings to this table," he began. "Both Alex and Richard have pointed out that while we've made strides, there are still areas that need our attention. But before we explore that, I want to acknowledge something."

He leaned forward and placed his hands on the table. "Our employee satisfaction numbers are up. In the middle of all this revolutionary change, that's nothing short of amazing. It's easy to keep folks happy when the sailing's smooth, but doing it now? That's a big deal."

The CEO paused, making sure his message hit home. "Your hard work has done this. The late nights, the constant championing of our strategy and execution method, the teamwork. It's all paying off. And it's not just numbers on a page – it's people feeling better about coming to work every day, even when the ground's shifting under their feet. We should all be damn proud of that."

He leaned back in his chair, taking a moment to scan the room. The soft hum of the air conditioning and the distant murmur of activity outside the conference room were the only sounds. His gaze met each of his team members in turn. He could see a glint of pride in their eyes.

"Alright," he continued, "let's move on. I want to touch upon our recent shift in governance structure. I'm aware it's been a significant change for all of us. Last month marked our first 'Initiative Deep Dive' session. Every department, every team, submitted their Key Activity plans for the coming quarter. They detailed their milestones and highlighted their most pressing tasks. As a team, we've reviewed every milestone of every critical initiative. It was no small feat. I'm keen to hear your reflections. Did the process feel overwhelming? Or did it offer the clarity we've been seeking?"

Margaret was the first to share her thoughts. "Our recent session was a departure from our usual meetings," she began. "The level of detail, the thoroughness of our discussions – for some of us, it was uncharted territory. On the upside, it fostered a stronger alignment across our teams, and we managed to identify and address potential challenges that could have cost us significantly in the long run. However," she paused, "it was intense. By the end of it, I felt drained. Over the years, we've had layers of management to navigate these intricate details."

Fiona chimed in with her perspective. "Maybe it's the engineer in me, but I've often felt our past management discussions were somewhat surface level. I'm not advocating for drowning in every tiny detail. I'm emphasizing the importance of those critical elements that are pivotal to a project's success or failure. In my view, last month's deep dive was a move in the right direction. We need to be fully engaged and grasp the nuances of our initiatives. Otherwise, we risk missing the game-changing details. And let's be clear, while we focused on milestones, there's a wealth of detail beneath them for those who wish to delve deeper. I believe we've found a balanced approach."

The CEO's brow furrowed slightly, a clear indication of the internal conflict he was experiencing. The clarity and alignment they had achieved in recent times were indeed something to be proud of, and so were the numbers. But a nagging concern persisted. Had they, in their pursuit of this clarity, unintentionally shifted the balance of power too heavily toward the management team? The idea of such a concentrated locus of decision making, with the management team as the sole epicentre, gave him pause.

Alex, sensing the CEO's introspection, decided to interject, his usual confident demeanour replaced by a hint of vulnerability. "Look, Fiona," he began, his voice slightly rougher than usual, "I've always been a big picture guy. Details? That was for others to handle. If it wasn't directly affecting my sales numbers, I didn't see the point in diving deep.

"But this new direction we took? It made me question my approach. I had to sit myself down and really think about how I've been doing things. Maybe it was time to change, to start paying attention to the smaller gears that keep the big machine running.

"I'm no scholar, and everyone here knows that. Heck, I've had my fair share of blunders because I missed some 'minor' detail." There was a collective chuckle from the room, a few recalling some of Alex's more memorable oversights. "But seeing the shift, feeling the energy change, and watching plans actually come to life? It's made me realize the value of being hands on during this change.

"And if getting into those details gets me a bigger bonus at the end of the year? Well, consider me a detail-oriented guy from now on!" The room erupted in laughter, appreciating the candidness and humour Alex brought to the table.

STRATEGIC GOVERNANCE

In the fast-paced world of corporate governance, the old adage 'time is money' couldn't be more relevant. Every meeting, every decision and every strategy we lay down is a testament to that. It might seem like we're caught in a never-ending loop of discussions and plans, but there's method to the madness.

It all boils down to getting it right from the start. Put in the time early for solid planning and aligning everyone on the team, and you'll sidestep a lot of backtracking and wasted effort later. Being smart with time now will save a lot more of it down the line. Think of it as calibrating your compass before you set sail. Nail your direction early, and you'll avoid veering off course later, making the whole trip a lot smoother.

As we think about the optimal strategic governance structure, envision a yearly wheel, a cyclical representation of an organization's strategic timeline.

THE YEARLY GOVERNANCE WHEEL:

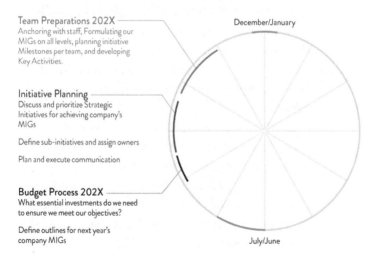

Team Preparations 202X
Anchoring with staff, Formulating our MIGs on all levels, planning initiative Milestones per team, and developing Key Activities.

Initiative Planning
Discuss and prioritize Strategic Initiatives for achieving company's MIGs

Define sub-initiatives and assign owners

Plan and execute communication

Budget Process 202X
What essential investments do we need to ensure we meet our objectives?

Define outlines for next year's company MIGs

December/January

July/June

1. *Budget Process (September/October of the Previous Year):*
   The beginning of the yearly cycle typically starts in
   the autumn of the preceding year. This phase is crucial as it sets the financial blueprint for the upcoming
   year. During this period, management teams should:
   • Discuss essential investments required to meet
     the company's objectives.
   • Define the outlines for the company's MIGs.

2. *Initiative Planning (October/November):*
   Post-budgeting, the organization's lens focuses on
   the intricate details that will form the backbone of
   the company's strategic direction for the upcoming
   year. This phase is pivotal in translating the broader
   objectives set during the budgeting process into
   actionable steps. Here's a more detailed look at the
   activities that dominate this phase:
   • **Re-evaluation and Prioritization of Initiatives:**
     Every initiative, whether new or ongoing,
     must align with the company's MIGs for the
     forthcoming year. This period is not just for
     adding new initiatives but also about critically
     assessing the current ones. There are times
     when the discussion simply reinforces the
     existing road map, but there are also moments
     when a complete overhaul is required. It's
     essential to:
     › Continuously evaluate the relevance of
       ongoing initiatives. Are they still in sync with
       the company's evolving goals?
     › Determine if certain initiatives have become
       part of the company's regular operations and
       no longer require the spotlight that a special
       initiative demands.

› Guard against the 'sunk cost fallacy.' It's crucial to objectively assess if continuing to invest in certain initiatives is beneficial. Just because resources have been poured into a project in the past doesn't mean it warrants further investment, especially if it's not delivering the expected value.

- **Detailing Sub-initiatives and Ownership:** Breaking down larger initiatives into smaller, more manageable sub-initiatives helps to ensure that every aspect of the project is addressed and can be clearly communicated. Assigning clear ownership for each sub-initiative encourages responsibility and accountability. It ensures that there's a dedicated person or team overseeing its progress, troubleshooting challenges and driving it to completion.

- **Strategic Communication:** An initiative, no matter how well-planned, can falter if not communicated effectively. This step prioritizes:

  › Clear and concise communication strategies that keep all stakeholders in the loop.

  › Alignment across departments and teams. Everyone should understand the 'why,' 'what' and 'how' of each initiative.

  › Updating stakeholders about progress, challenges and changes, ensuring transparency and fostering trust.

3. *Team Preparations for the Upcoming Year (Mid-November to Mid-December):*
As the year ends, forward-thinking organizations shift their focus to the horizon, laying the groundwork for the year ahead. This period, termed 'Team Preparations,' is instrumental in ensuring that the company starts the new year on the front foot. Here's a closer look at the activities that characterize this phase:

- **Anchoring New Initiatives and MIGs:**
  Before diving into the specifics, it's crucial to ensure that every team member is aligned with the new initiatives and the company's MIGs for the upcoming year. This involves:
  › Top-down communication about the rationale behind each initiative and goal, making sure that the 'why' is clear to all.
  › Engaging in discussions, addressing concerns and gathering feedback to ensure buy-in from all levels of the organization.
- **Formulating MIGs Across Levels:**
  While the company has its overarching MIGs, each department, team and even individual should have their own set of MIGs that align with and contribute to the company's broader objectives. This ensures that everyone has a clear direction and purpose.
- **Planning Milestones and Key Activities:**
  Each team should break down their initiatives into tangible milestones, plotting them out across the year. This involves:
  › Identifying key activities required to achieve each milestone.
  › Assigning responsibilities and setting deadlines so that progress is trackable.

- **Setting the Date for the First Strategy Stand-Up:**
  One of the most critical steps during this phase is
  to earmark a date early in the new year for the first
  Strategy Stand-Up. It's a common pitfall for many
  organizations to get caught up in the year-end
  frenzy, pushing planning for the new year to ...
  well, the new year. This results in a sluggish start,
  with January and even early February often lost in
  the post-holiday haze. By setting a clear deadline
  for the first Strategy Stand-Up, organizations can
  be ready to hit the ground running, maximizing
  their execution power right from the start.

  It's worth noting that while the preparation
  phase might seem intensive from an organizational
  standpoint, for individual teams, it boils down to
  just one or two focused meetings. Even amid the
  year-end rush, these sessions are not just feasible
  but essential. By investing this time in December,
  companies can effectively gain almost two additional months of productivity in the new year—
  a significant competitive advantage.

In essence, the Team Preparations phase is about proactive planning and recognizing that the best way to predict
the future is to create it. With this structured approach,
organizations are well-positioned to do just that.

INITIATIVE STEERING GOVERNANCE STRUCTURE:
After the initial planning and alignment phase, the
organization shifts into a rhythm of execution. Most of
the organization, equipped with clear directives from
the Strategy Stand-Ups, moves into execution mode. It
is focused on delivering results, driven by the clarity and
alignment provided by the management team.

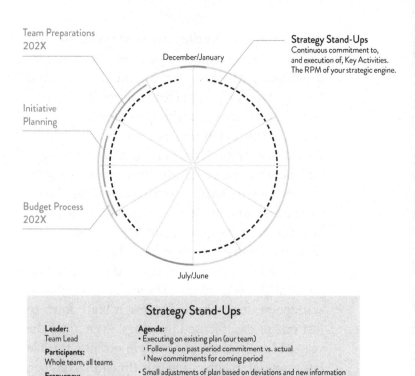

Team Preparations
202X

Strategy Stand-Ups
Continuous commitment to,
and execution of, Key Activities.
The RPM of your strategic engine.

December/January

Initiative
Planning

Budget Process
202X

July/June

Strategy Stand-Ups

Leader:
Team Lead

Participants:
Whole team, all teams

Frequency:
30 mins weekly/bi-weekly

Agenda:
• Executing on existing plan (our team)
  › Follow up on past period commitment vs. actual
  › New commitments for coming period
• Small adjustments of plan based on deviations and new information
• Discussion on risks/blockers from below
  › Take action via new Key Activity if needed

However, for the management team, the journey is more intricate. As stewards of the organization's strategic direction, their role is multifaceted. Not only are they responsible for setting the direction, they also focus on continuous alignment, evaluating progress and making course corrections. Their deep and ongoing planning and evaluation is crucial in ensuring that the broader organization's efforts are effectively directed toward the MIGs.

To manage this dual responsibility of strategic oversight and operational alignment, the management team relies on two primary meetings. These meetings, one looking forward and the other looking back, ensure that while the broader organization is in execution mode, the management team remains strategically engaged, ready to address both current challenges and future opportunities.

1. *Milestones Deep Dive (Looking Forward)*
   This quarterly meeting, led by the CEO, is a proactive planning session. It's about anticipating the challenges of the upcoming quarter and ensuring that the organization is well-prepared to tackle them.

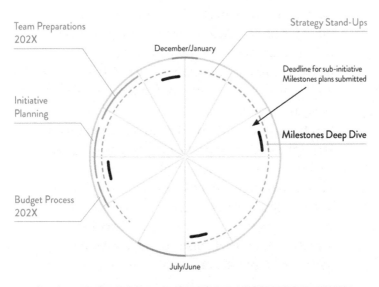

Team Preparations 202X

Strategy Stand-Ups

December/January

Deadline for sub-initiative Milestones plans submitted

Initiative Planning

Milestones Deep Dive

Budget Process 202X

July/June

Milestones Deep Dive (looking forward)	
Leader: CEO	**Agenda:** *When Management Team is steering the organization:*
Participants: Management teams *+Initiative owners if needed*	• Go through per initiative including relevant sub-initiatives › Make sure to understand Milestones in plan › Approve or challenge Milestones
Frequency: 3 hours quarterly	• Discuss what to do for organizational segments lagging › Take action via new Key Activity if needed

Alongside the management team, Initiative owners are also involved when their insights are deemed necessary.

Key Focus Areas:

- **Review of Initiatives:** A comprehensive examination of each initiative, including its sub-initiatives, ensures that the management team is well-versed with the upcoming challenges and opportunities.
- **Milestone Evaluation:** The milestones set for each initiative are scrutinized. They are either approved or challenged based on their alignment with the company's broader objectives and the feasibility of their execution.
- **Accountability Check:** Teams that are either off-track, lack a clear plan, or have a plan that doesn't align with the company's objectives are held accountable. This drives proactive planning and ensures that every team is aligned with the company's goals.
- **Strategic Interventions:** The management team strategizes on how to support and guide segments of the organization that might be lagging or facing challenges. To ensure timely interventions and corrective actions, Key Activities are added to the management team's Key Activity list. This structured approach ensures that issues are addressed promptly and effectively.

The success of this meeting hinges on preparation. Initiative owners are mandated to submit their plans in advance. To facilitate this, a proactive approach is recommended, such as distributing calendar invites highlighting the submission deadlines. This not only serves as a reminder but also emphasizes the importance of timely preparation. By marking these crucial dates, the management team's discussions are informed, focused and productive.

2. *Initiative Focused Strategy Stand-Up (Looking Back)*
   This monthly meeting, an extension of the regular Strategy Stand-Up for the Management Team, is for reflection and course correction. Led by the CEO, it's a time to evaluate the organization's progress over the past month, celebrate successes and address challenges.

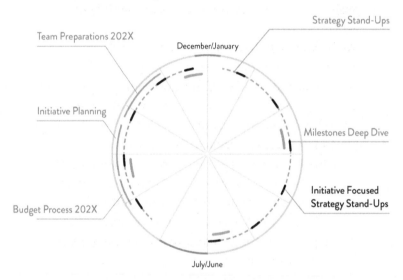

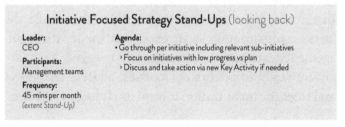

Initiative Focused Strategy Stand-Ups (looking back)

Leader:
CEO

Participants:
Management teams

Frequency:
45 mins per month
(extent Stand-Up)

Agenda:
• Go through per initiative including relevant sub-initiatives
  › Focus on initiatives with low progress vs plan
  › Discuss and take action via new Key Activity if needed

Key Focus Areas:

- **Performance Review:** The management team conducts a thorough review of each initiative and its associated sub-initiatives. This review not only provides clarity on the progress made but also highlights any challenges encountered. Instead of spending time on initiatives that are on track and executing as planned, the focus is primarily on those that are *off* track. This approach ensures efficiency, as there's no need to delve into well-executed plans unless there are significant learnings to share.

- **Addressing Challenges:** A proactive stance is taken toward initiatives that aren't progressing as anticipated. By identifying and addressing challenges early on, the team prevents minor issues from escalating into major obstacles.

- **Action-oriented Approach:** Building on the insights from the performance review, strategic interventions are identified, and tasks are assigned to the relevant members of the management team. These Key Activities are then monitored in subsequent meetings to ensure accountability and effective execution.

In essence, these two meetings ensure that while the broader organization is in execution mode, the management team remains strategically engaged. They are always ready to celebrate successes, address challenges and steer the organization toward its strategic objectives.

PART III

DIGITAL
ACCELERATION

As we move into the next phase, we're met with the transformative power of acceleration. We've explored strategy formation, and confidently navigated the realm of execution. We're now standing on the precipice of harnessing the digital revolution's full potential.

Imagine a seasoned sailor in a race, skilled in navigating both turbulent storms and calm seas, suddenly surrounded by the noise of engines and much faster competition. This isn't the familiar territory of old, where traditional sails and compasses sufficed. The horizon has shifted. The crew, once reliant on maps and stars, now faces a world where modern technologies set the pace.

In today's business landscape, where change is the only constant, strategy is the dynamic force that drives an organization. Making decisions in the boardroom is one thing; but implementing those decisions across the organization is another. Traditional tools like Power-Point or consultant-aided models are too static to handle the rapid pace and breadth of change we face. We need digital tools that offer not just real-time updates, but also the scalability to manage widespread transformation. These tools are indispensable for orchestrating complex change and ensuring that every part of the organization moves in harmony toward its common goals.

In this final section of the book, we begin by spotlighting the evolving role of the CEO in the digital epoch. Recognized as the last analogue executive, the CEO emerges as the transformative figure pivotal to this revolution, underscoring the imperative for leadership that champions technological advancements. Subsequently, we delve into the Evolution of Strategic Software, emphasizing its potential, and examine the indispensable role of digital tools in strategy deployment within our accelerated business landscape.

But as we embark on this digitally charged journey, remember the mission we set out with at the beginning: to not just be bystanders, but to be trailblazers in this transformative era. I invite you to embrace the revolution, the pace and its transformative potential. Together, we'll not only decode the nuances of digital strategy, but also set a new gold standard for what can be achieved. As the business landscape morphs, we won't just adapt; we'll lead, daring to think differently and act boldly, redefining the future of strategy execution.

CHAPTER 8

THE LAST OUTPOST AND THE CEO AS THE LAST ANALOGUE EXECUTIVE

Imagine a CFO in a world without financial systems; hunched over a desk, quill in hand, painstakingly recording debits and credits into a hefty ledger. The endless hours spent cross-checking, the furrowed brow searching for that one elusive error. Imagine corridors filled with rows of bookkeepers, scribbling away, trying to keep pace with the relentless demands of modern financial reporting.

Now, shift your gaze to the Sales Manager's office. Instead of sleek CRM systems, you find a cluttered desk with a rolodex spinning endlessly. Fax machines whirring as contracts are sent out, and sales activities summarized as handwritten notes. The absence of digital marketing strategies, lead generation tools, sales funnels and opportunity boards paint an archaic picture.

Yet, here's the twist in our tale: the life of a modern CEO closely mirrors this antiquated scenario. Granted, they're not entirely cut off from the digital world. Emails ping constantly, and virtual meetings have become second nature. They can summon a plethora of Business Intelligence (BI) reports at a moment's notice. But these tools, while useful, only skim the surface.

This disconnect is underscored by recent findings from Accenture,[13] revealing a paradox at the core of corporate strategy. Despite CEOs recognizing the urgent need to address this business challenge, only 5% of organizations are fully leveraging tailor-made software in strategy execution. This statistic not only highlights a missed opportunity but also indicates a huge issue: the reliance on traditional tools, while familiar, restricts their capability to manage the complexities of strategic planning and execution. They choose instead to maintain an alarmingly analogue approach in a progressively digital world.

Join me on a journey along the winding roads of digitalizing strategy. The journey typically starts from the familiar realm of PowerPoint. Whether birthed in the hallowed halls of elite strategy consultancies or echoing the remnants of a whiteboard brainstorm, the corporate strategy usually springs to life within the confines of a slide deck.

This deck, adorned with charts and bulletpoints, becomes the Swiss Army knife of strategy communication. It's paraded in boardrooms, disseminated to mid-tier managers, and often morphs into templates that local leaders grapple with, trying to tailor them to their unique challenges. Occasionally, Excel makes an appearance, its grids and charts attempting to capture the ebb and flow of strategic progress. Traffic light indicators paint a rosy picture, with green lights aplenty, lulling one into a false sense of security. That is, until the deadline looms, and the lights suddenly flash red, signalling unmet targets and unfulfilled promises.

Enter the tech aficionados. These companies, in their quest for digital nirvana, attempt to graft strategy modules onto their sprawling ERP systems, hoping to seamlessly blend strategy with execution. Strategic Initiatives are drowned amid the cacophonous din of daily operations.

The crux of the problem lies in the absence of a unified strategic nerve centre. Instead, strategies scuttle about, residing in disparate documents, each with its unique flair and format, stashed away in the recesses of local drives – picture the frantic scramble to locate the 'final-final-v2' version of a document.

INCREASING PRESSURE ON CEOS

In a bygone world where business as usual was the norm, strategy was often a slow-moving giant. Transformations took time, often years. But the winds of change are blowing far more quickly. With disruptions becoming almost an annual event, the weight on a CEO's shoulders has never been heavier. While having a digital snapshot of daily operations is a step forward, attempting to shoehorn strategy into the framework of BI has revealed its limitations.

In the BI universe, data is meticulously collected and housed in expansive warehouses. These systems excel at diving deep, transitioning from overarching views to granular details, helping us decode our historical trajectory. But consider strategy execution in the BI system in the analogy of a GPS: it's adept at recounting where we've been, but falters in knowing where we're going. Even data labelled as 'real-time' is only a reflection of actions and decisions made months ago. It's a delayed echo of past endeavours.

Boards, stakeholders and the market at large demand not just innovation, but swift, tangible progress in these new directions. This urgency is compounded by an era marked by unprecedented disruptions, technological advancements and shifting consumer behaviours.

The pressure isn't just about reporting progress; it's about making meaningful strides forward, often in environments rife with uncertainty and volatility. For CEOs to lead effectively, they need a clear view of the road ahead, equipped with insights that offer foresight, not just a reflection of what's been left behind.

THE MIRAGE OF FINANCIAL PROMISES

As the CEO's role is transitioning and becoming more pressured, the clarity of their strategic view becomes crucial. Yet, within many organizations, this view is obscured by 'beautified' data reporting. Managers often highlight the successes while omitting less favourable outcomes, and it is this selective reporting that leads to a skewed understanding of performance.

The responsibility then falls on the senior executives to discern the full picture. They must possess an encyclopedic memory, recalling not just the overlooked KPIs but their intricate details, milestones and deadlines. They must spot inconsistencies and ask uncomfortable questions. This isn't just for one direct report, but perhaps for eight or more. The role morphs from a strategic overseer to a relentless inquisitor, constantly pushing and doubting. It's not just mentally taxing but emotionally draining.

As these polished reports climb the corporate ladder, they gain layers of optimism. By the time they reach the CEO, ready for presentation to investors and boards, they're often a far cry from the ground reality. This embellishment is costly. *Harvard Business Review* reveals that companies typically achieve only 63% of their projected financial growth,[14] a testament to the high price of looking good. Over time, such trends erode trust in the CEO, and can ultimately be detrimental for career advancement.

This issue is compounded by strategic plans built on 'hockey-stick' projections – cautious growth in the near term with ambitious leaps in later years. Yet, as the initial conservative years pass without the expected trajectory, strategies are often reset. New plans with recalibrated goals emerge, still predicting steep inclines in the future. It's a cycle of revision and overpromise, masking past underperformance with new, optimistic forecasts.

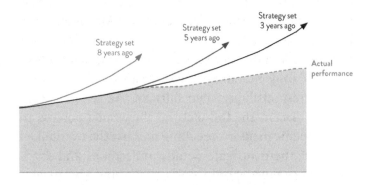

For a CEO guiding a company through change, relying on such data is like navigating with a faulty compass because conventional KPIs offer limited insights too late. Senior leaders need real-time progress insights to address bottlenecks and resistance effectively, beyond what they can typically access in their ERPs or BI-systems. It's vital to cultivate a culture of transparency and realism, where strategies and reports reflect the true situation, allowing for alignment with the actual terrain and aiming for sustainable growth. The speed that leaders can pinpoint and resolve execution roadblocks is crucial, because it directly impacts the success or failure of their strategic implementation.

Leaders must leverage the right tools – those that cut through the fog of embellished data and provide a clear view of the company's strategic landscape. As we turn the page on outdated practices, let's explore available software solutions that are evolving the art and science of strategy.

THE EVOLUTION OF STRATEGIC SOFTWARE TO SIMPLIFY GROWTH

One of the bigger drawbacks for the advancement within this field is that traditional software companies often lack a deep understanding of CEO scorecards, focusing instead on operational tasks at the expense of high-level strategic goals. The focus has typically been on optimizing for incremental improvements with a team-centric approach, without the right support for organization-wide strategic transformations or behaviour change. Ultimately, this leads to fragmented strategies that miss the big picture. While these applications boast considerable flexibility, this very attribute can lead to an excess of customized governance models within an organization, breeding confusion and multiple, disconnected methods of execution.

Historically, strategy consultants have been instrumental in aiding CEOs during periods of change. However, the challenges faced by management consultancies in this context largely arise from their fundamental structural and operational models. Traditionally, these firms are oriented toward a project-based, client-specific service approach, heavily focused on tailoring solutions to meet individual client requirements. The issue is that offering guidance on an hourly basis is not scalable across an organization – you'll never achieve the critical mass necessary for impactful change. While these consultants excel in strategy development, delegating execution to consultants is a very expensive way of getting things done in the 21st century.

This has left too many senior leaders still juggling with PowerPoint and Excel to manage their company's strategy. They're playing by an old playbook in an updated game.

As we navigate through the evolution of strategic software, we're active participants in a revolution. An Execution Revolution that promises to transform the intricate task of driving growth from a complex challenge into a simplified discipline. The next generation of strategic tools doesn't just assist; it propels us forward. Modern software not only simplifies the pursuit of growth, but ensures that every strategic decision is informed, every action is deliberate, and every result moves us closer to our vision.

THE DAWN OF DIGITAL STRATEGY EXECUTION

The early platforms for strategy execution were like the first cars – functional, but not particularly efficient. Barely more than cloud-based Excel models, they were reactive, often lagging behind the fast-paced world of business.

But as the winds of change blew, a new wave began to form. This wave believed that merely monitoring outcomes wasn't enough. The focus shifted to optimizing the inputs that would lead to better outcomes.

The terms 'lead and lag KPIs' emerged. A leading KPI represented the activity that would lead to a goal, while a lagging KPI measured the outcome of that goal. But there was a catch. To truly understand these KPIs, a bottom-up approach was needed alongside the traditional top-down method. This meant that everyone had to be involved in the strategy formation.

Books and thought leaders of the time began to emphasize the importance of agility in strategy execution. The idea was to adapt frameworks from the IT world, where teams integrated regular check-ins to plan deliverables and review past achievements. This approach brought more accountability and reduced planning horizons. However, while it increased efficiency, it was still time-consuming, and the thirst for a faster method was palpable.

From the limitations of the first wave, two parallel approaches surfaced:

1. *Software supporting the OKR Methodology*
   The Objectives and Key Results (OKRs) methodology, popularized by industry titans like Google, promised a revolution in strategic alignment and clarity. By setting lofty objectives and measurable key results, the intention was to synchronize every level of an organization with its core aims. This method, when applied effectively, could transform a company's trajectory, infusing every task with purpose and direction.

   As the allure of OKRs spread, specialized software platforms sprang up to support their implementation, offering features to track progress and foster company-wide alignment. The proliferation of these tools signalled a shift toward a more structured approach to strategy within diverse sectors.

Yet, the journey toward OKR proficiency has revealed critical pitfalls. A notable challenge has been maintaining true alignment across an organization. Teams, while successful in achieving their own OKRs, often struggled to integrate their goals with the broader company vision, leading to a fragmented strategy where departmental success might not translate to overall progress.

Furthermore, the aspirational nature of OKRs has sometimes led them astray. The methodology's encouragement of 'stretch goals' has, in some instances, resulted in objectives that are more aspirational than practical – goals that are marked 'complete' because of their subjective nature more than any measurable impact. This 'fluffiness' can dilute the potency of actions, leading to a complacency where the drive for tangible change is replaced by a sense of achievement in merely aspiring.

Lastly, organizations, in their zeal to set goals, often underestimated the complexity involved. This underestimation, coupled with a failure to prioritize effectively, led to goal inflation. Instead of a few clear, impactful objectives, teams found themselves drowning in a sea of targets, many of which lacked the strategic importance or the alignment the OKR methodology championed.

In essence, although the OKR methodology and related software tools provided a hopeful route toward strategic clarity and alignment, their effective implementation often fell short due to a fundamental misunderstanding of the underlying business issues.

Many organizations attempted to digitize goal management without fully grasping its intricacies. It's like purchasing a car without knowing how to drive – owning the vehicle doesn't guarantee you'll reach your destination.

2. *Task Management Approach*
The alternative approach adopted by organizations was turning to task management systems already embedded in their daily operations. Platforms like Jira, Trello, Notion and Microsoft Planner gained traction. Their appeal lay in their adaptability; teams could mould these tools, creating custom boards that mirrored their strategic aspirations, integrating these goals seamlessly with routine tasks.

This adaptability was both a blessing and a curse. On the one hand, teams could tailor these platforms to their unique needs, ensuring that day-to-day operations and strategic goals were in sync. But on the other hand, this very customization often led to a muddled landscape where high-impact strategic tasks jostled for space amid a sea of routine, low-impact tasks. The result was often a skewed perception of progress. Teams might celebrate a 95% task completion rate, not realizing that the crucial 5% – often the challenging strategic tasks – were left untouched.

Moreover, while these tools excelled in enhancing the efficiency of individual teams, they faltered when it came to providing a unified, organization-wide view of strategy execution. Each team, with its custom board and set of tasks, became an island. Much like the problems with PowerPoint strategy decks, the broader organizational objectives, which should have been the guiding star, often got obscured in this archipelago of team-specific goals.

In essence, while task management tools offered a promising avenue for integrating strategy with daily operations, they often fell short in driving holistic, organization-wide change. The challenge lay not in managing tasks but in ensuring that the right tasks – those that aligned with the overarching strategic vision – were prioritized and executed.

TOOLS FOR THE CEO

The demands for strategic progress and transparent reporting have never been higher. This has naturally led to a growing need for digital tools tailored specifically for executive leadership.

At the core of this evolution is the need for alignment. The best modern tools are designed to echo the CEO's vision, ensuring that the broader strategy is consistently applied throughout the organization. It's about making sure everyone, from top-tier management to frontline staff, is moving in the same direction.

Another key aspect is the emphasis on true priorities. In a world filled with distractions and a constant barrage of 'urgent' tasks, these tools help managers and their teams focus on what's genuinely important. Especially when there's a shift in direction, it's crucial that the time from decision making at the top to execution at grassroots level is minimized. This isn't just about speed; it's about survival in a disruptive environment.

Execution, however, isn't just about tasks and targets. It's about people. Even if strategy execution is deeply complex to master, it's crucial that the roll-out of any technical or methodological support does not impede the adoption process, slowing down the overall pace of strategic implementation. A tool can have all the features in the world, but if it's not user-friendly, it becomes more of a hindrance than a help. Organizational change is challenging enough without adding complex systems into the mix.

The goal is to provide tools that are intuitive, making the process of change smooth and efficient. Simplicity, therefore, is not just a feature; it's a catalyst. Remember that post-decision, CEOs require rapid, organization-wide execution, turning strategy into immediate action.

Here, the right tools step in, offering support structures like regular check-ins or 'Strategy Stand-Ups' and visual aids that showcase real progress, while keeping the team motivated and aligned with the bigger picture.

The onus is now on software developers and providers to not only create a tool, but to understand and address the real-world challenges of CEOs and their organizations. The digital strategy tool landscape is evolving rapidly. While there's no one-size-fits-all solution, the trend is clear: tools that offer clarity, alignment and simplicity are leading the way.

In every field of expertise, technologies and methodologies progress to meet the demands of the era. Just as a carpenter wouldn't revert to a basic hand drill when state-of-the-art electric drills are at hand, a surgeon wouldn't contemplate using a hacksaw, reminiscent of a time when absinthe was the primary anesthesia. In the same vein, it's impossible to understand why business leaders, entrusted with guiding vast organizations through today's dynamic landscape, would even contemplate depending on antiquated tools, ill-suited for their task.

A study published in the *MIT Sloan Management Review*[15] sheds light on this critical aspect. Surveying around 2,000 companies, the study found a stark disparity in performance linked to digital competence at the top level. Only 7% of these companies were led by digitally competent teams, where at least half of the members possess a firm understanding of how emerging technologies shape their company's success.

These digitally savvy companies demonstrated remarkable superiority, outperforming others by 48% in terms of revenue growth and market valuation. The era of the analogue CEO is drawing to a close, and there's a definitive call for CEOs to evolve. The findings from the study are unequivocal: CEOs who adeptly utilize digital tools to augment their role not only manage to survive; they excel, propelling their organizations to unprecedented levels of performance.

As a CEO, it's your prerogative to choose the tools and systems that will shape your organization's future. I understand the challenges you face – when you seek input from your team, you often steer toward flexible, operationally focused software that ultimately keeps the status quo. But here's the thing: you have a unique vantage point, the overarching vision that no one else in your organization possesses. This is me, speaking directly to you, giving you the nudge, perhaps even the permission you need, to stand firm against any skepticism from your team about adopting new ways of working and more advanced tools that align with your strategic agenda.

You're not just a decision maker; you're the guardian of your organization's evolution. It's not merely about exerting authority; you're embracing the responsibility that comes with your position.

To every CEO reading this: trust your instincts. If you see the need for change, for modern tools that resonate with your strategic needs, it's within your right to push for them. It's about leading with conviction, knowing that the success of your organization rests on your shoulders. Don't shy away from being the catalyst for change. Your ability to say, "We need this" and lead the charge, even when it's easier to maintain the status quo, is what sets you apart. Embrace the tools that empower you to lead effectively.

CHARTING THE DIGITAL FRONTIER

While this book doesn't endorse any specific software, the underlying message is clear: CEOs must equip themselves with the most advanced and suitable tools available. It's not just about keeping up with the times; it's about being effective, efficient and visionary. It's a journey that demands courage, adaptability and a commitment to continuous learning. But for those who embark on it, the rewards are substantial.

My journey has been one of deep immersion in the intersection of strategy and digital innovation. Witnessing firsthand the costly missteps of flawed execution, I've dedicated myself to the digital vanguard of strategy execution. I'm not interested in chasing trends; my focus is on catalysing a fundamental enablement of a better world, where we collectively achieve more of what matters to us.

I imagine a future where the untapped potential of organizations is harnessed, where groundbreaking innovations are brought to fruition, and where global challenges are met with decisive and effective action. This is the future I am passionate about helping to create – a future where the principles of strategic clarity, focus and actionability turn into the norm, fuelling progress that benefits businesses, society and the planet.

For those curious about the digital frontiers I navigate and the solutions I advocate, I invite you to explore beyond the confines of this book. The Execution Revolution is not just a topic I write about – it's the professional crusade I embark upon every day, driven by the belief that with the right tools and mindset, we can simplify growth and amplify impact.

CHAPTER 9
THE DESERVED BREAKTHROUGH

In the calm of the backstage lounge, a world away from the grandeur of the conference centre's main stage, the management team found solace. This tranquil space, with its subdued lighting and plush sofas, offered a stark contrast to the bright lights and intense scrutiny they had just left behind. Here, the team could absorb the significance of what they had just accomplished.

Laughter and soft conversations filled the air, as each member relished in a sense of achievement. They gathered in an informal circle, their bond deepened by the trials and triumphs they had shared.

Maximilian, the CEO, stood in contemplation. He wasn't just thinking about the presentation they had aced or the applause that still rang in his ears from the shareholder meeting they'd just concluded. His thoughts were on the journey that had brought them here. He thought about the days when their company, now lauded in financial circles, was just another struggling entity in a sector beset with stagnation and challenges.

Revolutionary was the word that came to mind when he considered their transformation. From the brink of obscurity to posting growth figures that echoed the industry's golden era, their success was testimony to their relentless execution and strategic effort. It wasn't luck or a single masterstroke that had turned their fortunes around; it was a collective resolve to reinvent themselves and boldly embrace change.

There was a time when Maximilian was viewed with skepticism, even by the chairman. Competent but unremarkable, his leadership hadn't always inspired confidence. But now, as he stood amid his team, he felt a sense of vindication. The organization's upward trajectory could redefine his legacy, transforming him from a competent CEO to a visionary leader.

He glanced around at his team, each member absorbed in their own reflections and quiet celebrations. Maximilian knew that their achievements went beyond internal improvements. They had made a tangible impact, translating their strategic ambitions into real business growth. It was a validation of their hard work, a testament to the power of focused goals, aligned teams and the right digital tools.

MOST IMPORTANT GOALS

Joining his team, he said, "You know, genuine victories are few and far between in my experience. Reflecting on our strategy retreat 18 months ago, we faced a crucial juncture. The progress we've made since then, by focusing on what actually matters, is astounding."

Margaret, mirroring Maximilian's thoughtful demeanour, added, "That retreat definitely marked a significant shift. It taught us that chasing after everything only leads to achieving little. Embracing the MIGs transformed our approach."

Alex chimed in, "Focusing on fewer, yet vital things made all the difference. We cleared the clutter to spotlight our essential growth drivers. And it went beyond goal setting. We aligned every team member's efforts, and created a shared sense of purpose and empowerment."

"One aspect I thought would be more challenging was handling the goals we set aside," Maximilian said.

Richard's eyes lit up with a spark of enthusiasm. "Exactly, while we have a multitude of objectives, we only earmarked a few as 'Most Important.' It's like a car's dashboard, where only critical metrics like the fuel gauge or speedometer are in constant view. The rest stay in the background, coming into focus only when necessary. This analogy really helped us refine our goal management method."

"My finance team's experience mirrors this," Richard continued. "We're always monitoring various metrics and addressing anomalies as they arise. Sometimes, these deviations become temporary MIGs, but once resolved, we refocus on our primary strategy. This balance of vigilance and efficiency has been really helpful."

"Our achievements are a testament to this focused approach," said Maximilian. Making tough decisions and fully committing to them has been crucial. And Fiona, your insights on our Strategic Initiatives have been pivotal. What would you say was the most important lesson from that experience?"

STRATEGIC INITIATIVES

Fiona, attentively engaged in the conversation, shared her thoughts. "I believe our Strategic Initiatives were pivotal in bringing everything together. Goals are just aspirations without concrete plans. Essentially, we're discussing the engines that are driving our MIGs."

She continued, "It's easy to get lost in buzzwords like automation, sustainability and innovation. We've sometimes fallen into this trap in the past, but we made a concerted effort to add substance to these concepts. Breaking them down into smaller, manageable sub-initiatives was vital, each contributing meaning-fully to our larger strategic objectives."

Maximilian, acknowledging her point, added, "Absolutely. Breaking down complex initiatives into actionable components was crucial. Vague Strategic Initiatives hinder execution. Our approach provided a clear and robust framework, allowing us to transform our goals into a growth road map."

Richard nodded, "And we can't overlook our focus on prior-itizing quality over quantity. It ensured that every initiative was the pivotal force we needed to significantly impact our goals."

Margaret reflected, "The way we tackled these initiatives cross-functionally played a huge role. By aligning every depart-ment with the same objectives, we ensured a unified approach to our strategic journey."

Maximilian, looking around at his team with pride, remarked, "The clarity we achieved in our Strategic Initiatives and their exe-cution has been integral to our success. It's about more than being aspirational or narrowing our focus. We now understand which levers to pull and we've been putting all our organizational force behind those pivotal initiatives."

KEY ACTIVITIES

"If there's one thing that truly transformed our approach, it's the concept of Key Activities," Alex began. "I'm all about action, and this is where theory turns into practice. It's the practical side of our MIGs and Strategic Initiatives."

"I think it's remarkable how everyone in our company, from interns to senior managers, understands exactly what they need to do to advance our goals. That's the level of action-orientation our Key Activities brought us," he added thoughtfully.

Margaret nodded in agreement. "You're absolutely right. And let's not forget how it forced us to have those tough but necessary team conversations. We had to pinpoint actions that were outside our comfort zones but essential for real progress, tasks that have a positive impact on our MIGs."

Fiona said, "It was about instilling a sense of ownership, wasn't it? More than just aligning with our goals, we have made everyone feel they were actively contributing to the journey, connecting their day-to-day actions to the broader company strategy."

Maximilian reflected on the initial hesitations from different teams. "I recall our internal discussions about the pushback. Some perceived this new clarity as micromanagement," he mused. "But we knew that we had to focus on high-impact activities. Once we communicated the principle that a small number of activities drive most of our results, and the importance of identifying and optimizing these Key Activities, the mindset began to shift. Building an organizational model that prioritizes and rewards these activities set us on the path to success."

"That's true," Alex said, "and it wasn't always an easy journey. Guiding our managers to embrace this shift involved belief in our methods and the need to confront resistance. But our steadfast commitment and resilience as a team have been remarkable. Let's not forget the elephant in the room. Our sector's been taking hits. So, what? We just sit back and watch the show? Once you see what not making bold calls does, any other way just seems like a waste of time."

STRATEGY STAND-UPS

"We're actually overlooking one of our most transformative practices," Fiona pointed out. "As Alex rightly said, it's the execution that really counts. And for us, Strategy Stand-Ups have been a critical element of that process."

Maximilian nodded, keenly aware of their impact. "Yes, the Strategy Stand-Ups have been like a weekly gas pedal for our organization, haven't they? A rhythm that kept us aligned and accountable."

Fiona agreed, "Every Monday morning, it's almost like a ritual. Each team across the company takes 15-30 minutes to reflect and plan. The first part is about looking back – did we meet our commitments from the previous week? Then, we focus on the future, committing to specific Key Activities for the week ahead. But I know that for my teams, it has become more than just a meeting; it's a chance for leaders to focus their teams on what's most important above the daily shuffle. Focus-driven, week in and week out. And it gives us the ability not just to monitor progress but truly drive behaviours through the commitments."

Richard interjected with a note of admiration in his voice. "The beauty of this process is how it resonates throughout the company, from the ground level to the management team. It's that kind of accountability that's been instrumental in navigating our challenges."

Maximilian agreed, "Every Monday, I sense the collective heartbeat of our organization, all moving in unison toward our goals. Purpose and action. That, to me, is the real power of unwavering commitment and unity. It's something that fills me with immense pride."

DIGITAL ACCELERATION

Maximilian then shifted the discussion to the impact of their digital tool. "Honestly, there's no way we could have got the impact or kept our momentum within our massive organization without a huge leap in digital maturity. It's been a game-changer for scaling our efforts and complex strategy to so many people, without diluting it or losing sight of its progress."

Margaret agreed. "The tool has been more than a digital aid; it's the backbone of our new way of working. It unified our approach and provided clarity. Now, everyone understands what matters the most and how we're progressing. The level of visibility it's given us across all levels has been exceptional."

Richard highlighted the tool's practical impact. "It's transformed abstract strategy into something concrete while scaling it across numerous teams. Our business reviews from just a year ago were a reel of endless slides and hours of preparation, often leaving us more confused than informed. Now, the clarity, focus and actionability we've achieved with this tool far surpass what we ever managed with traditional methods."

Alex pointed out the efficiency gains. "My teams have stopped manually aggregating data from our CRM systems for reports. Often, the strategic information we needed wasn't even available. CRM data mostly catered to our operational side, revealing little about our strategic progress. It was such a tedious process for managers to compile the necessary information. This tool has brought us such simplicity – what a relief."

Richard returned to the financial aspect. "While I understand the benefits of a simpler reporting process, the true value of this tool is its ability to spot misalignments, blockers or resistance. From our calculations, having the ability to intervene early on has contributed to significant cost savings from quicker, more effective execution."

"I completely agree with you, Richard," Maximilian said. "The introduction of a single source of truth within our management team has significantly improved our meetings. We're no longer bogged down by trying to interpret real progress from overly-polished presentations; instead, we can concentrate on planning our next steps. This shift has eliminated the lack of strategic focus that used to lead us into missed opportunities and reactive decision making. We avoid getting sidetracked by trivial details, effectively maintaining our role as the guardians of long-term value while actively driving our organization forward. Spending our time on what really matters has been fantastic for me."

"On a personal note," Maximilian began, "my interactions with the board have also become much smoother. Since we've aligned on our strategy, including our MIGs and Strategic Initiatives, if I can demonstrate clear progress on these initiatives and address any shortcomings, there's a complete trust that the financial outcomes will follow suit. And so far, they have. This approach has granted me more autonomy and bolstered the trust in our discussions."

THE CULMINATION OF CONVICTION

As the team dispersed, their laughter and words of congratulations were punctuated by handshakes, cheerful pats on the back and satisfied smiles. Each person went home with a sense of achievement and a renewed commitment to their shared journey.

Eventually, Maximilian found himself alone. He allowed himself to fully absorb the magnitude of their achievements. This wasn't merely a triumph of goals met or expectations surpassed; it was the result of boldness and vision. A sense of pride swelled within him. They had all dared to venture where others hesitated, challenging the norms and rewriting the rules. This was more than success; this was a legacy.

With a deep, contented breath, Maximilian savoured the moment of triumph. This journey had embodied the very essence of their mantra, to focus on less to achieve more. They had sparked the Execution Revolution within their organization, a transformation that promised not only to redefine their future successes, but also to serve as a beacon for others. This was their legacy – not just meeting targets, but pioneering a new way forward, proving that with conviction and the principles of the Execution Revolution, the extraordinary was within reach.

AFTERWORD

Kudos for making it through this book. But for you, that's just the starting line, not the finish. Now, you've got to ask yourself a pretty important question: Are you actually going to act on what you've learned, or are you going to be one of those leaders who nods along but never makes a move? I've seen too many smart people recognize their flawed ways, yet they do squat about it because they're scared of a little pushback. Don't be that person.

Take a hard, honest look at your current practices. Are they really up to snuff in our hyper-competitive world? If you're hesitant to admit there's a problem, you're already falling behind. Need a hand figuring it out? Remember the assessment option we discussed. My team and I are here to help, especially if you're running a significant operation – but let's be clear, only reach out if you're truly ready for a change.

Do you have a management team? Good. Hand them copies of this book and dive into it. Commit to the four concepts – Most Important Goals, Strategic Initiatives,

Key Activities, Strategy Stand-Ups. Going all-in is key; cherry-picking the easy stuff is a safe but ineffective strategy for most endeavours worth pursuing. And keep in mind, focusing on less to achieve more isn't just a catchy phrase; it's the best way to contribute to the Execution Revolution in your own ecosystem.

Don't overlook your own behaviour. If you're treating strategic planning as someone else's job, you're dropping the ball. Strategy isn't a spectator sport; it's your game and you're the star player. Look back at last week's calendar. How much time did you dedicate to proactively driving your strategy forward? It should be a logbook of proactive strategizing, not just a series of meetings where you react to the present. Get a grip on your schedule. Carve out the hours and guard them with your life. Be the operational driving force behind your strategy. Don't delegate the future.

Now, let's talk about your legacy. It's not about crossing off goals but what you leave behind. If you're just coasting along, afraid to make waves, what kind of legacy is that? It's time to step up, make those tough calls, and stop being content with 'good enough.' You've got the chance to rewrite the playbook – what are you waiting for?

Resistance? Sure, you'll get plenty of it. But here's a newsflash: as a leader, it's your job to cut through that. You've got the broad vision that no one else has. So, when your team pushes back on adopting new methods or tools, remember, you're the one at the helm. It is your mandate to push through the inertia and skepticism. Be the leader who drives change, not the one who shies away from it.

Let's talk digital maturity. Honestly, the level in many senior teams is just too low. It's not necessary to master every new gadget or app, but you do need to understand how digital tools can amplify your strategy by giving it scalability. If you're dragging your feet on this, wake up. The longer you resist, the harder it will be to catch up. And believe me, catching up is a hell of a lot harder than keeping pace.

I know I've been pretty straight with you throughout this afterword. Call it tough love, but I firmly believe that sugarcoating won't serve you or your company. However, this doesn't diminish my genuine gratitude for your willingness to engage with these ideas and my hope for what you will accomplish.

On that note, I want to sincerely thank you for picking up this book. I hope the candour has sparked a fire and prodded you into action. I wrote this for you. Seize this moment. Embrace it, and let's start trailblazing. Don't get left behind as the world moves forward. The future waits for no one.

Good luck, and let's make some waves!

Johan

CORE CONCEPTS LEXICON

MOST IMPORTANT GOALS (MIGS)

WHY

The relentless drive for success often leads organizations to scatter their focus and chase every emerging opportunity. This fragmented approach squanders precious resources and dilutes the potency of efforts, resulting in subpar outcomes.

In contrast, the distinguishing trait of high-performing teams is their sharp focus. They understand that resources are finite: every chosen project comes at the expense of another; every minute invested in one task is a minute withheld from a different, potentially more impactful activity.

Mastery of the art of saying 'no' is not about being negative; it's about strategically choosing where to channel the organization's invaluable assets: time, energy and resources. Neglecting this principle results in a frenzied, ineffective strategy that barely impacts the organization's trajectory.

WHAT

MIGs are not just any goals; they are the select few that are critical for business improvement. These are the goals that, if achieved, will have the most significant impact on the organization's success.

- **Less is More**

  The principle of 'focus on less to achieve more' guides the selection of MIGs. Limiting each team to 2-3 MIGs ensures that resources and attention are not spread too thinly, increasing the likelihood of successful execution.

- **Hierarchical Alignment**

  Each team's MIGs should be directly aligned with the goals of the team immediately above them in the organizational hierarchy. This maintains a focused and coherent strategy as goals cascade through the organization.

- **Accountability and Influence**

  Teams should select goals that fall within their direct sphere of influence. This means that team members will feel accountable for the outcomes, fostering a sense of ownership.

- **Measurability**

  MIGs should be measurable, ideally monthly, and align with the SMART goals framework (Specific, Measurable, Achievable, Relevant, Time-bound).

HOW

To effectively implement MIGs, an organization must embark on a structured prioritization journey, commencing at the highest level of leadership:

- **Senior Leadership Initiative**

  The top management starts by defining and prioritizing the organization's MIGs, leveraging their comprehensive view and authority to initiate the prioritization process.

  The focus is narrowed from a broader range of goals (5-20) to a concise set (2-3), establishing a clear direction for the entire organization.

- **Departmental Alignment**

  Each management team member, often overseeing their profit and loss responsibilities, conducts workshops with their teams to understand and decide how they can contribute to the broader MIGs. This collaborative approach encourages ownership and aligns the teams' unique capabilities with the organization's strategic objectives.

- **Cascading Goals**

  The process of aligning and interpreting MIGs continues down the hierarchy, with each manager facilitating discussions within and across teams. This step ensures that all levels of the organization understand and are committed to the MIGs, promoting focus and strategic coherence.

- **Review and Refinement**

  After the entire organization has engaged in setting and understanding the MIGs, the executive team reviews the outcomes to ensure alignment with the intended strategic focus. This phase addresses any deviations from the original strategy, resolves cross-functional dependencies, and makes sure that the implementation stays on track.

OUTCOME

By following this top-down and bottom-up approach, every team within the organization ends up with their set of MIGs that support the overarching organizational goals. The outcome is a clear goal map that illustrates the interconnectivity of objectives across all levels, defining responsibilities and showing the direct line of support for each MIG. This unified structure replaces the multitude of conflicting goals with a streamlined, focused strategy, enhancing the organization's ability to execute and achieve its MIGs.

STRATEGIC INITIATIVES AND SUB-INITIATIVES

WHY

Strategic Initiatives are the bridge from ambitious financial goals to tangible results, representing the 'big bets' that can pivot a company's direction and significantly influence its performance, accounting for over 45% of corporate performance variance. These initiatives extend beyond incremental improvements, which typically sustain the status quo. Instead, they embody the strategic decisions that concentrate effort and resources on a select few high-impact areas, offering a real chance to surpass organic growth.

WHAT

Strategic Initiatives serve as actionable pathways designed to realize the MIGs and illustrate HOW we plan to achieve our objectives. These initiatives provide a transparent growth road map, pinpointing sources of performance enhancement. These initiatives make the strategy understandable for everyone in the organization, concentrating efforts and making clear the rationale behind your strategic direction. Through Strategic Initiatives, you specify the steps and measures needed to translate the strategic vision into tangible results, aligning all efforts with the main goals.

Strategic Initiatives should:
- **Enable your MIGs**
  For each of your primary goals, you'll have specific initiatives to help you achieve them.
- **Be Prioritized**
  Typically, you'll have 3-6 initiatives supporting your set of 2-3 MIGs.
- **Have Financial Potential**
  When you add up the potential of all these initiatives, they should help close the financial gaps between your current trend and your strategic budget.

For every Strategic Initiative you choose, you should be clear about:

- **Purpose and Objectives**
  Why is this initiative important, and what do you hope to achieve with it?

- **Sub-initiatives**
  These are smaller, more specific projects within the main initiative. The principle of priority still holds true when deciding on your sub-initiatives.

- **Responsible Teams**
  Identify which teams or departments will oversee the carrying out of each sub-initiative.

HOW

Implementing Strategic Initiatives requires a methodical approach, beginning with the identification of key levers that will propel the organization toward its strategic vision:

- **Senior Leadership Direction**
  The C-suite starts by distinguishing between incremental improvements and Strategic Initiatives. Their role is to envision and set in motion the few pivotal interventions that promise a significant shift in performance.

- **Strategic Selection**
  From a broader list of potential initiatives, the management team selects a focused set that represents the best opportunities to impact the MIGs. This involves a balancing act between ambitious leaps and achievable steps

- **Initiative Breakdown**
  Each Strategic Initiative is dissected into sub-initiatives, making them more manageable and enabling specific teams to take ownership of discrete components of the strategy.

- **Resource Allocation**
  Decisions on resource allocation prioritize Strategic Initiatives, ensuring they receive the necessary attention and investment to succeed.
- **Milestone Planning**
  The owner of each Strategic Initiative is tasked with designing and seeking approval for a series of ambitious milestones. These milestones are crucial for ensuring that each initiative contributes to the MIGs in a timely and effective manner, keeping the overall strategic plan on track.
- **Key Activity Planning**
  Following milestone planning, individual teams involved in the initiative develop detailed Key Activity plans. This step integrates top-down strategic direction with bottom-up insights, ensuring that the execution is grounded in practical actions. It leverages the expertise of those closest to the work, aligning their day-to-day activities with the strategic milestones.
- **Monitoring and Adaptation**
  Regular reviews of progress against Strategic Initiatives allow for adjustments and refinements, ensuring alignment with evolving strategic objectives and external conditions.

OUTCOME

Adopting Strategic Initiatives as described aligns the organization's efforts toward achieving its most ambitious goals. It transforms strategic planning from a theoretical abstract into a practical, focused action plan. By concentrating on a limited number of Strategic Initiatives and making sure they are equipped with clear, ambitious milestones, companies can channel resources effectively, enhance organizational alignment, and significantly improve the chances of outperforming their underlying market.

KEY ACTIVITIES

WHY

Achieving significant goals isn't just about measuring the outcome; it's about zeroing in on the crucial activities that propel us toward these goals. The essence of success in any endeavour, like the often-cited examples of diet and exercise in personal fitness, lies in focusing on controllable, impactful actions. This focus on actionable steps, rather than the result, is where true progress is made. Many organizations lose sight of this, getting entangled in the allure of the end goal without anchoring their efforts in the activities that lead there. This concept is about moving focus toward real life execution, moving from dreaming into doing.

WHAT

Key Activities are identified as the pivotal actions with the most substantial impact on achieving your goals. These are not just routine tasks, but high-leverage activities that directly influence the success of the organization's MIGs. Key Activities offer a way to focus efforts and resources where they are most needed, providing clear direction on what actions are pivotal for the team and the organization. However, it's crucial to note that prioritizing Key Activities is not about micromanaging every minor task. This approach would be impractical and, ultimately, counterproductive. Instead, the goal is for teams, in alignment with overarching company goals and initiatives, to pinpoint a select number of impactful actions. These Key Activities then serve as the foundation for steering the team's efforts and monitoring their progress toward strategic success.

A Key Activity is an action that combines both qualitative and quantitative aspects. It's structured around four essential components:

- **Title**
This acts as the identifier for the activity. It's designed to be succinct, memorable and distinct, setting the Key Activity apart from routine tasks. Unlike typical tasks that might be input-oriented, a Key Activity's title emphasizes the desired outcome and the progress it aims to achieve.

- **Purpose (Description)**
This provides the reasoning for selecting this activity. It acts as a reminder of the strategic thought process that led to its inclusion. Essentially, it explains the business objective the Key Activity aims to fulfill.

- **Definition of Done**
This is the benchmark for the Key Activity. It specifies the standards that need to be achieved for the activity to be marked as completed. Activities that meet this criterion contribute toward the team's goal, ensuring alignment with the team's MIGs.

- **Recurring Numeric Goal or Deadline**
This component sets the rhythm. It quantifies the amount of the Key Activity required weekly to significantly influence the MIG, or the deadline by when it must be done.

By adopting this structure for Key Activities, teams can ensure that every step they take is deliberate, meaningful and directly helps to realize the team's MIGs.

HOW

1. **Identify the MIGs**

   Begin with a clear understanding of your team's MIGs. Focus discussions on identifying actionable steps your team can take to effectively achieve these goals. It's about moving from the 'what' to the 'how' in practical terms.

2. **Organize a Brainstorming Session**

   Hold a brainstorming session with your team to generate ideas for Key Activities that can contribute to achieving the MIGs. Encourage openness and creativity, welcoming all suggestions. The objective is to identify controllable actions that directly impact your goals.

3. **Groom Your Idea List**

   After brainstorming, refine your list to include only actionable inputs that your team can directly influence. This step narrows your focus to activities that are both actionable and impactful toward achieving the MIGs while emphasizing your team's ownership for improvement.

4. **Prioritize Impactful Activities**

   Prioritize actions based on their impact, sidelining activities that would happen organically. Employ voting or consensus to distill the list to the most impactful Key Activities, ensuring focus and effective resource allocation.

5. **Define Key Activities Clearly**

   Clearly define each chosen Key Activity, adhering to the outlined structure of Title, Purpose (Description), Definition of Done and Recurring Numeric Goal or Deadline. This clarity moves you away from vague intentions and toward accountability and specific action – both of which are crucial for catalysing action.

6. **Embrace Challenge and Act Proactively:**
   Motivate your team to undertake these activities, especially those that stretch their capabilities, as these often yield the most substantial growth. Highlight the importance of being proactive, tackling challenging tasks, and focusing on impactful activities for significant progress toward strategic goals.

OUTCOME

Following this structured approach not only clarifies the actions required to achieve strategic goals but also empowers every team member to actively engage and contribute to the organization's success. By embedding this methodology into the fabric of your organization, you cultivate a culture of commitment and understanding, where everyone understands their role in the broader strategic context, and their responsibility in turning goals into reality. This significantly enhances the organization's ability to execute its strategy by scaling these efforts across all levels.

STRATEGY STAND-UPS

WHY

The greatest challenge in strategy execution isn't the lack of direction but the relentless pull of daily operations that consistently sidelines long-term goals. This whirlwind of immediate tasks and urgencies has a powerful tendency to push strategic Key Activities to the perpetual 'next week,' undermining the organization's ability to achieve its MIGs. Without a deliberate mechanism to counteract this force, pivotal improvements are perpetually deferred in favour of more pressing, but often less impactful, day-to-day demands. The need for active steering arises from this very challenge – ensuring that Key Activities are not just identified but consistently prioritized, protected from the whirlwind's sway, and advanced week after week. This active, focused management is crucial for transforming strategic plans from intention to action, maintaining momentum, and ensuring that the organization's strategic vision is realized in the face of operational demands.

WHAT

Strategy Stand-Ups are short, weekly meetings (15-30 minutes) designed specifically to bridge the gap between strategic intentions and tangible actions. These meetings focus exclusively on progress toward the team's MIGs, emphasizing the Key Activities. The structure of Strategy Stand-Ups encourages transparency, accountability and a shared commitment to collective goals, turning them from burdensome tasks into a cohesive effort toward common objectives. They serve as a sanctuary from the daily chaos, a dedicated time to focus solely on actions that move the needle toward achieving strategic milestones. These meetings also help to align team members and foster accountability.

HOW
Setting Up Strategy Stand-Ups:
Organize a dedicated weekly Strategy Stand-Up meeting, distinct from regular team meetings. This separation safeguards MIGs and Key Activities from the overshadowing effect of operational matters. It's recommended that you allocate the first segment of a longer meeting exclusively for the Strategy Stand-Up, followed by a separate segment for operational discussions.

Preparation Phase (5-10 minutes before the meeting):
- **Team Leader Preparation**
  Assess the previous week's commitments against actual progress. Make a note of any deviations or unmet commitments. Consider tactics for offering support or guidance.
- **Team Member Preparation**
  Consider what Key Activities need attention in the upcoming meeting, highlight blockers or share new insights. Prepare to discuss specific commitments for the week.

During the Strategy Stand-Up:
Team Leader's Role:
- **Progress Overview**
  Begin by summarizing the team's progress toward the MIGs, emphasizing the importance of these goals and discussing any necessary adjustments of the plan to meet the goals.
- **Celebrate Success and Learnings**
  Highlight successes from the previous week and share insights beneficial to the entire team.
- **Focus on Key Activities**
  Identify Key Activities requiring additional focus, emphasizing accountability and the importance of follow-through on commitments.

- **Active Engagement**
  Listen attentively as team members share their commitments, taking notes to track progress and support needs.

Team Member's Role:
- **Commit to Key Activities**
  Clearly articulate the Key Activities you plan to tackle in the coming week, specifying the actions you will take and the expected timelines.
- **Contribute to Discussion**
  Engage in a conversation about progress and learnings, offering insights or suggestions that may benefit the team's strategic efforts.

OUTCOME

Adopting Strategy Stand-Ups is a powerful method for leaders to maintain a laser focus on strategic priorities, foster accountability, and delineate strategic pursuits from the distraction of daily operations. This approach ensures that long-term goals are not just another item on the agenda but are the central focus of the team's efforts. By making individual commitments a core part of these Stand-Ups, every team member, from interns to the CEO, becomes a direct contributor to the organization's strategic objectives.

Furthermore, Strategy Stand-Ups instigate a profound transformation in organizational culture, where focus, accountability and strategic alignment are not just valued but are embedded into the fabric of everyday work. These sessions keep everyone aligned with the organization's goals and are part of a culture where commitment to strategic success is a shared responsibility across all levels.

DIGITAL ACCELERATION

WHY

The challenge in executing strategy across an organization isn't merely about setting goals. It's vital to ensure that these goals resonate and are actionable at every level. Traditional tools like PowerPoint and Excel, while familiar, are inherently static and disconnected, and fail to engage the broader organization in a meaningful way. The problem lies in scaling strategy effectively – rapid dissemination, uniform understanding and coherent action is necessary across all teams. Without a unified approach, strategic efforts become fragmented, leading to inefficiencies and missed opportunities.

WHAT

Digital tools for strategy execution represent a paradigm shift from traditional, analogue methods to a dynamic, interactive approach. These tools enable organizations to quickly roll out strategic changes, maintain alignment across all levels, and actively steer toward goals rather than merely monitoring progress through backward-looking metrics. Unlike static presentations or spreadsheets, digital platforms offer real-time updates, collaborative features, and the ability to adjust tactics promptly based on current performance.

HOW

- **Recognize the Digital Imperative**
  Understand that the digital maturity of leadership teams is often insufficient for the complexities of modern strategy execution. Moving beyond traditional tools to digital solutions is essential for scalability and agility in Strategic Initiatives.
- **Select Appropriate Digital Solutions**
  Choose a digital platform that offers clarity, alignment and simplicity. It should support the setup of strategic goals, allow real-time progress tracking, and facilitate Strategy Stand-Ups for continuous alignment.

- **Implement for Alignment and Agility**
  Deploy digital tools that support every team member's understanding of their role in the strategic plan. Utilize these tools to break down goals into actionable Key Activities, and to make sure that strategic imperatives are clearly communicated and integrated into daily operations.
- **Promote a Culture of Active Steering**
  Enforce the use of digital tools across the organization. Distinguish between monitoring (passive observation of outcomes) and steering (active management of inputs to influence future outcomes). Digital tools should be used not just for tracking performance but for guiding teams toward strategic actions and effective follow-through.

OUTCOME

Implementing digital tools for strategy execution significantly boosts an organization's ability to effectively scale and manage its strategic endeavours. By providing a centralized, digital framework for strategy management, organizations can move beyond inefficient traditional methods to achieve a unified and focused approach to strategic advancement.

Digital strategy tools offer a real-time overview of strategic progress, facilitating swift identification and resolution of misalignments or resistance. This visibility enables more effective execution and leads to significant cost savings. Furthermore, these tools cultivate a culture of transparency and accountability, ensuring that progress toward strategic goals is openly monitored and communicated.

The adoption of these tools also brings efficiency gains by reducing managerial workloads, eliminating the need for manual data aggregation, and shifting the focus to strategic activities. For leaders, digital tools improve communication with both teams and superiors by centring discussions on tangible, actionable data. This approach helps bypass the embellishment of results and concentrates dialogue on priorities, thereby enhancing decision making and strategic focus.

REFERENCES

For quotes not attributed to a specific source, they are widely recognized sayings that have been associated with the named individuals through their public speaking engagements and are commonly found in the public domain.

1. **Jimmie Butler.** *"90 Percent of Organizations Fail to Execute Their Strategies Successfully,"* IntelliBridge. https://www.intellibridge.us/90-percent-of-organizations-fail-to-execute-their-strategies-successfully/

2. **Project Management Institute.** *"$1 Million Wasted Every 20 Seconds by Organizations around the World,"* PMI.org. 2018. https://www.pmi.org/-/media/pmi/documents/public/pdf/about/press-media/press-release/pulse-of-the-profession-2018-media-release.pdf

3. **Jenny Davis-Peccoud, Michael Mankins and Jeff Denneen.** *"Managing Initiative Overload,"* Bain & Company, March 6, 2014. https://www.bain.com/insights/managing-initiative-overload/

4. **Donald Sull, Rebecca Homkes and Charles Sull.** *"Why Strategy Execution Unravels – and What to Do About It,"* Harvard Business Review, March 2015. https://hbr.org/2015/03/why-strategy-execution-unravelsand-what-to-do-about-it

5. **Chris Bradley, Martin Hint and Sven Smit.** *"Strategy to Beat the Odds,"* McKinsey & Company. February 7, 2018. https://www.mckinsey.com/capabilities/strategy-and-corporate-finance/our-insights/strategy-to-beat-the-odds

    Carolyn Dewar, Martin Hirt and Scott Kelle. *"The Mindsets and Practices of Excellent CEOs,"* McKinsey & Company. October 2017. https://www.mckinsey.com/capabilities/strategy-and-corporate-finance/our-insights/the-mindsets-and-practices-of-excellent-ceos

6. **Donald Sull, Charles Sull and James Yoder.** *"No One Knows Your Strategy — Not Even Your Top Leaders,"* MIT Sloan Management Review. February 24, 2015. https://sloanreview.mit.edu/article/no-one-knows-your-strategy-not-even-your-top-leaders/

7. This reference brings together insights from a variety of research, each pointing to similar trends in strategy execution. Here is a selection of some of the key studies that support these findings:

    *   **Brent Gleeson.** *"1 Reason Why Most Change Management Efforts Fail,"* Forbes, July 25, 2017. https://www.forbes.com/sites/brentgleeson/2017/07/25/1-reason-why-most-change-management-efforts-fail/

- **John Kotter.** *"What Happens When the Strategy Consultants Leave?"* Forbes, January 4, 2012. https://www.forbes.com/sites/johnkotter/2012/01/04/what-happens-when-the-strategy-consultants-leave/

- **Michael Beer and Nitin Nohria.** *"Cracking the Code of Change,"* Harvard Business Review, May-June 2000. https://hbr.org/2000/05/cracking-the-code-of-change

- **Greg Gerstenhaber and Hernan Saenz.** *"Bending the Cost Curve,"* Bain & Company, 2019. https://www.bain.com/insights/bending-the-cost-curve/.

- **Jackie Wiles.** *"The Five Pillars of Strategy Execution,"* Gartner, 2023. https://www.gartner.com/smarterwithgartner/the-five-pillars-of-strategy-execution

8. **Rich Horwath.** *"The 3 Disciplines of Strategic Thinking,"* ISE Magazine, August, 2020. https://www.isemag.com/professional-development-leadership/article/14267335/the-3-disciplines-of-strategic-thinking

9. **The Economist Intelligence Unit.** *"Why Good Strategies Fail: Lessons for the C-suite,"* Project Management Institute, 2015. https://www.pmi.org/-/media/pmi/documents/public/pdf/learning/thought-leadership/why-good-strategies-fail-report.pdf

10. **Michael E. Porter and Nitin Nohria.** *"How CEOs Manage Time,"* Harvard Business Review, July-August 2018. https://hbr.org/2018/07/how-ceos-manage-time

11. **Rich Howarth.** *"The Strategic Thinking Manifesto,"* 2012. https://www.strategyskills.com/pdf/The-Strategic-Thinking-Manifesto.pdf

12. **Simon Elvnäs.** *Effektfull: Detaljerade Studier av Ledarskap – Så Ökar Du Effekten av Din Tid.* Volante, 2020.

13. **Accenture.** *"CEOs Identify Combination of Data, Technology and People as Future Growth Driver, Yet Only 5 Percent of Organizations Realizing Its Value,"* Newsroom, January 17, 2023. https://newsroom.accenture.com/news/2023/ceos-identify-combination-of-data-technology-and-people-as-future-growth-driver-yet-only-5-percent-of-organizations-realizing-its-value

14. **Michael C. Mankins and Richard Steele.** *"Turning Great Strategy into Great Performance,"* Harvard Business Review, July-August 2005. https://hbr.org/2005/07/turning-great-strategy-into-great-performance

15. **Peter Weill, Stephanie L. Woemer and Aman M. Shah.** *"Does Your C-Suite Have Enough Digital Smarts?"* MIT Sloan Management Review. https://sloanreview.mit.edu/article/does-your-c-suite-have-enough-digital-smarts/